CUBICLE COMMANDO

Lisa Messenger & Zern Liew

First published in 2006

Messenger Publishing
PO Box H241 Australia Square NSW 1215
www.messengermarketing.com.au
www.eicolab.com

National Library of Australia Cataloguing-in-Publication Data:

Messenger, Lisa; Liew, Zern

Cubicle Commando: intrapreneurs, innovation and corporate realities.

1st ed. ISBN 0 9775519 0 3

1. Entrepreneurship. 2. Creative Ability in Business. 3.Technological Innovations -
Management. 4. Organizational Learning. 658.4

Concept and initial ideas: Lisa Messenger, Zern Liew and Paul Morris

Design:	Eidesign www.eidesign.com.au
Marketing and PR:	Messenger Marketing www.messengermarketing.com.au
Editing:	Whyte ink

Produced in China through Bookbuilders

To all the intrapreneurs and entrepreneurs who are out there setting the trends and breaking the rules, and who remain a constant source of inspiration to us.

To all the spirited people and organisations working against mediocrity; and doing the right thing by themselves and their community.

And to all the naysayers who push us on, because whenever you say we can't, you're just daring us to show you we can!

The status quo no longer has "status"

If you joined a big company looking for protection and prestige, I hate to be the bearer of bad news, but you will be sadly disappointed. Today, start-ups don't hold a monopoly on revolutionary thinking. The big boys have also learned the business-rebel tango. Over the course of a few decades, Nokia morphed from manufacturing boots for the military to becoming the world's leading telecommunications equipment manufacturer. More recently, Apple moved from being an also-ran in the personal computer hardware space to being at the front of the pack for how the world purchases and listens to music in the 21st century. Status quo has become status go!

So, what does it take to be a rebel in a big company? That's what Lisa and Zern are going to tell you in this intrapreneur's manifesto. They've done a masterful job of pointing out that there's an art and a science to making a difference in a big company. It takes a certain amount of chutzpah, mixed with careful planning and thoughtful relationship-building. If I think there are two qualities that most define the successful intrapreneur, they are authenticity and courage.

In the old days (we're probably talking 30 years ago at this point), if you wanted to climb the corporate ladder, you became the master of the false smile. Getting to the top was more about looking good (and knowing the right people) than being good. And, it certainly wasn't about being yourself, as the upper echelons of management were full of empty suits who'd deposited their souls at the door when they got to work each day.

Today, we all appreciate candor and individuality more than ever before. In a world full of imitation and replication, what stands out is what's rare. And, what's rare in big companies (although becoming less rare) is authenticity. "Being real" is a breath of fresh air in an overly air-conditioned corporate world. Original thinking, genuine human connection, and a willingness to respectfully speak out – those are some of the authentic qualities that define the most effective intrapreneurs in the workplace today. Like a moth to a flame, we want to be near people who clearly are "being all they can be."

That last quality, a willingness to respectfully speak out, amplifies the other quality – courage – that is an essential attribute of the Cubicle Commando. Historically, we've thought of the entrepreneur as the courageous one while those who joined a big company were taking the safe path. But today, big companies that are wedded to being safe are becoming roadkill. We live in too competitive a worldwide economy with way too much change and innovation for anyone to rest on their laurels. So, intrapreneurs who are willing to stick their neck out are becoming increasingly powerful in big companies.

Many of us have some outdated idea of what a courageous person looks like, such as someone willing to go into the outback with merely a knife and canteen of water for a week. Let's shift your thinking, as the bar you have to jump over to be courageous isn't nearly that high. The number one quality that defines courage in a big company is the willingness to ask the question, "Why?" Most people just accept things the way they are. They assume there's some corporate logic that overrides their opinion. Or, worse yet, they feel apathetic because they truly don't believe their voice means anything.

Just ask, "Why?" Make a pact with yourself that you'll ask this question five times a day. "Why are we continuing to advertise on that TV station?" "Why don't we have a head of innovation in this company?" "Why don't we pay our superstar employees much higher compensation so they don't get stolen away by the competition?" "Why are we in this particular business?" There's courage in the question "Why?" There's also innocence, because children ask this question ten times as much as adults do. So, when you're asking why, do it from a place of innocence and authenticity, as opposed to sounding purely disagreeable or difficult. I promise you, Nokia and Apple are asking why all the time.

In sum, the best advice I can give you is to enjoy yourself. Move from being a Cubicle-Codependent who's just trying to fit in to being a Cubicle Commando who takes delight in making a difference in the world and provides a role model to those around them. Good luck on your journey!

Chip Conley
Founder & CEO
Joie de Vivre Hospitality

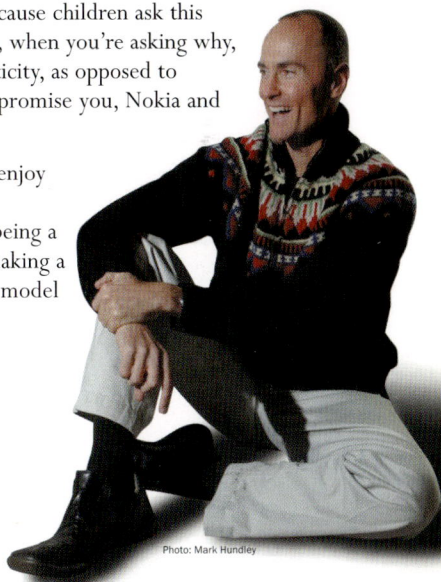

Photo: Mark Hundley

Hi from the authors!

Cubicle Commando evolved largely as a result of our own frustrations. We have witnessed and experienced the internal battle of intrapreneurs from all angles.

When we encounter a problem, in true entrepreneurial fashion, we can't help but tackle it and shake things up along the way.

As individuals who have an unwavering belief that anything is possible, we thought it was our duty to share some of the wisdom and funky ideas that we have developed through our years in the various facets of business – from working for corporations, to sitting on Boards, to having our own companies.

Our vision was to create a book to reflect our higher purpose, with the aim of connecting like-minded people, to recognise and celebrate the intrapreneur in business, to reward the best thinkers, and work towards defeating mediocrity.

To give you an overview of how this book evolved, following are some notes drafted from our initial visioning session.

We hope our vision has been realised, and you can now share in our journey.

Lisa & Zern

**What's in a name?
Cubicle Commando –
assonance, action, irreverence,
maverick, fun, funky, freedom.**

Working title:

Cattleprod

Vision

Create a book that completely changes the way people think; challenges and takes them out of their comfort zone.

To push the barriers, to be controversial, edgy and innovative. To push entrepreneurship and free spirit in any job or situation

To get people to start thinking for themselves and being creative.

To not regurgitate the same old stuff. Readers must want more of this!

To create a cult-like phenomenon; a media frenzy!

Bring together two like-minded "young" Australians from both sexes to shake things up a bit.

Would be great if we become "the leaders" in Australia for completely changing the corporate culture!

Make this book part of the curriculum in schools, TAFEs, universities as well as for business leaders.

Anti-monetary and materialistic greed – a much more holistic approach to business – redefine success and associated values!

Anti wanker. Anti ego.

To take it internationally to showcase Australian innovation in business thinking.

See it translated into multiple languages.

Make this a "ding!" moment book. Penny dropper. Provides clarity for those who already think this way, reading the book in their cubicles.

Draw together fellow cult members – bringing together people who already think like this. We are not alone.

To have people quoting from it everywhere!

Target market

People who are open to change and evolution, and who are prepared to do whatever it takes.

Age? – probably not an issue – more so a mindset – people evolve at different times.

Wider audience, not necessarily just intrapreneurs.

Thinkers and mavericks.

Key messages

How readers will feel when they read the book:

Challenged, invigorated, passionate, blown away, pushed to the limit, ready to take on the world, not scared to take risks, pumped up!

No longer needing to play it safe. Skip out of their comfort zone!

Showing them that there are different ways of thinking and there is more than one way to do anything.

That they can have work, life, philanthropy and that it all sits side by side and works; harmoniously flowing through all aspects of their life.

Their values, visions and beliefs should be reflected in everything they do (why do they change when they go to work?)

Wow. Cool.

I am not alone.

Rethink how to do business at a fundamental level.

Integration of life-work. Integrated whole self in both work and life.

Anti-formula. Anti-establishment. Connect to self; not just another mindless cog.

A key to a whole new world.

Objectives

Make a difference.

Have fun.

Learn lots.

A book that creates a stir; that slaps people in the face.

Fundamentally unique. Not just by design.

Personal pride. A momento.

Extremely sexy to look at, a pleasure to touch, a breeze to navigate and a delight to read.

Prove that a successful business woman does not have to be a bitch or have no life.

Prove that a successful business man does not have to be an emotionless and soulless bean counter and hoarder.

Prove that a successful business can meet all the numerical criteria for silly awards AND still do cool stuff.

Actions we want readers to take

Start thinking big, not being constrained by tradition, being aware that there is another way.

They will be full of ideas and passion for their new direction, and will seek out fellow travel companions and mentors.

Become part of a cross-organisational cultural change movement. Start to change the way corporates think from within.

Positioning

THE Tom Peters of Australia!!!

Change -drivers.

The anchovy of business books.

Unique Value Proposition

We are young.

We are living this – we have lots of examples to back it up.

We have the track record.

We have a good mix of fun and business.

It is written by both male and female.

Two young Australians from different backgrounds.

Soul and meaning. Part of the wider wellbeing movement. People buy as a statement of their personality.

Unique content, not a rehash.

Has substance, not just being different for the sake of it, for fashion's sake. Not just an attention grabbing tagline.

Endorsed by gurus and everyday unknown people.

Stating things clearly and without corporate speak.

Calling a spade a spade. Cut through the crap.

Genuinely empowering for the individual. Not a lecture. With actions an individual can take, even if this is a change in thinking.

Introduction

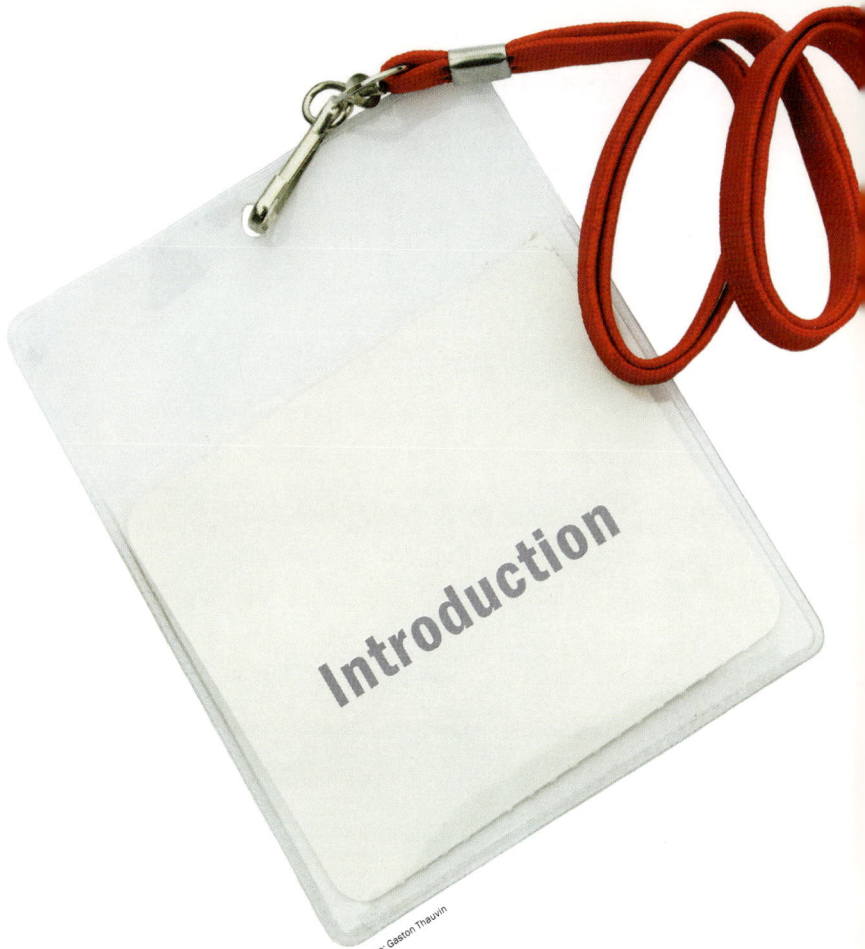

Business is the engine room

Like it or not, business, especially big business, powers the world, and shapes our lives. Government policies and religions are giving way to commerce as the driver of the majority of changes in our world. Not that money in and of itself is the answer – it isn't. But money can mean opportunity, choice and freedom, like never before.

Basically, nothing extraordinary (in terms of moving mankind forward and cleaning up some of the world's mess) happens unless sanctioned by business – money drives everything. That's why people like Bono and Bob Geldof are working with economic forums and business groups in an effort to drive the changes that are so desperately needed throughout the world.

We have to engage in some way with business every day – whether as an employee, a consumer, an employer, a supplier, a regulator, or simply as a citizen feeling the impact of the activity (or inactivity) of businesses.

Corporations have largely replaced the communities of old, but many are failing to accept the accompanying responsibility to provide for the emotional, spiritual and social needs of their members.

Because business has such a broad global influence, poor decisions and unethical actions can have enormous and long-lasting impact. We hear a lot of talk about corporate social responsibility, family friendly workplaces, balanced scorecards and green business. Unfortunately, most businesses are still operating under the same factory model they've been using since the industrial revolution. The basis for decision-making and measuring success is still predominantly the bottom line.

The business landscape has changed, and continues to change at an accelerating rate. The world is becoming smaller, the playing field is being levelled. Commoditisation of everything is rife. Anything that can be systemised is being outsourced to low-cost providers in countries such as India and China, so we have to find new areas of competitive advantage. We're moving from the knowledge age to the conceptual age, where the need to be creative, innovative, and flexible is paramount.

Too much decision making is driven by short-term timeframes such as electoral cycles and CEO contracts, with insufficient thought for, or courage shown in addressing, long-term considerations. Everyone talks innovation, though too often the reality is more about minor improvements, maintaining the status quo, and ensuring that short-term bottom-line goals are achieved at least expense and with least change.

A lot of what business, especially big business, is doing is not good. But what can we do to change things? True, we can turn our backs, boycotting the multi-nationals, waging protests, trying to ignore or avoid the problems. But there's another way. We're talking about working inside the tent to drive change – leading by example in showing big business that there's a better way to operate, a way that is good for everyone – now and in the future; about leveraging its undoubted power for good, for sustainable profit and for the future of the planet. We're talking about the power of AND.

Photo: Dawn Allynn

Have your cake and eat it too!

It can be done most of the time if we are creative about it. And we practice inclusiveness and sharing. And avoid outright greed.

The power of AND is about win-win situations for all stakeholders in any venture. It is a great manifestation of "working with constraints" and "working within systems" to achieve results that have benefits for the system as well as the other stakeholders. Examples of the power of AND in business are: ethical produce – where farmers get paid a decent wage and consumers get a great product.

Another example is the rise of culture change programmes within corporations that attempt to encourage innovation and creativity, and to foster meaningful work within the ranks, to staunch the outflow of creative people.

The world of business today

Sea of same – or should that be shame?

So many businesses today are just carbon copies of each other. They operate the same way, they're managed the same way, they hire the same people to produce the same goods and deliver the same services; all to the same industry standards. So many executives perform like wind-up clockwork toys, marching to the beat of an increasingly irrelevant drummer towards the same end. No wonder mediocrity rules.

Too many businesses have just one goal: to make LOADS of money. There's nothing wrong with wanting to maximise shareholder returns – by definition, profit-making is the reason businesses exist. But there are ways and there are ways.

Often the easiest and least creative ways involve slashing costs, exploiting people, and plundering the environment. Such short-term, reductionist thinking is unsustainable, and can cripple organisations and ultimately the world in which we live. How many celebrity CEOs have ridden into town and immediately slashed and burned to produce some apparently impressive (short-term) turnaround results, only to leave behind a floundering basket case as they ride off into the sunset with their hefty 'performance' bonuses tucked safely into their saddle bags?

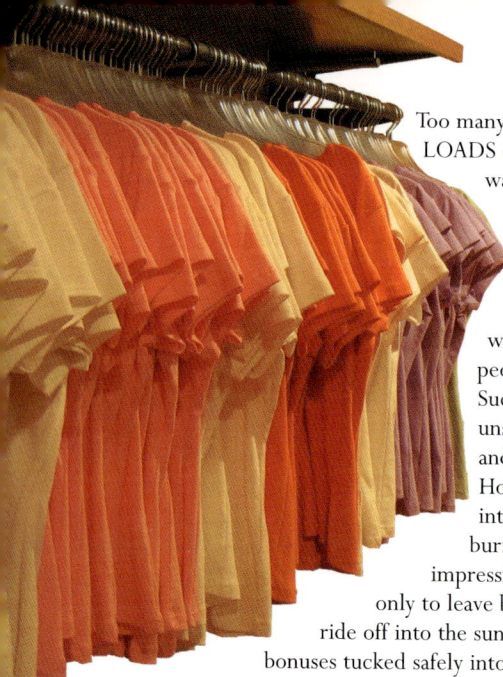

Photo: Zern Liew

So what happened to freedom?

Democracy, personal freedom, and the opportunity to engage in capitalism, aka business, has come to be seen as the preferred option to alternative ways of organising societies, such as communism, socialism and dictatorships. But all too often, we see that businesses have no soul. They're hijacked by those who view them as a tool to make money for the few at the expense of the masses. The rich become richer, while the poor become increasingly dis-enfranchised.

Unfortunately, too many businesses are controlled by unimaginative, one dimensional, egotistical, greed-driven people. Their minds are closed to innovation. They're always looking over their shoulder, driven by fear. They get so caught up in their own hype, taking it, and themselves, all too seriously, that they can't see the forest for the trees. There's no fun, no sense of, let alone celebration of, community and creativity.

Our mission is: to be the leading expert on anything and everything; to be the market leader anywhere and everywhere; to care for our valued customers through excellent and cheap customer service; and to increase shareholder returns above all else.

The people who work in these organisations are largely viewed as cogs in some immense, anonymous machine. They have no sense of purpose or meaning. They forget their values and what's important to them. They're programmed to live someone else's life. They sell their lives to organisations to make money so they can buy things they don't need to impress people they don't like. How ironic. That doesn't sound much like freedom.

Shaking it up

Subversion in business is important. The alternative is mindless acceptance of mediocrity. It's so sad to see genuinely creative people being exploited, apparently willingly. Not good enough! To question everything, to challenge the way things are done, is to provide the spark for creativity and innovation that's necessary for survival.

Business is a paradox, in that on the one hand, it's a simple process of exchange – I give you value, you give me value in return. But it's not quite as straightforward as that, because those strange and wondrous creatures, humans, are involved. Which is why things tend to get a little crazy.

The fundamental thinking of the Re-imagine! approach focuses on five themes:

Passion, the outward expression of intensity, belief and values.

Disruption, a discontinuity in a business model, caused by external or internal forces.

Risk, a requirement for innovation.

Entrepreneurship, cherishing independent thinking and individual innovation.

Re-imagination, fostering breakthrough ideas for organizational transformation.

Tom Peters Company, tompeterscompany.com

Conventional business is too focused on operational details like the latest management and IT fads; total quality management, just-in-time manufacturing, cost management (read cutting), knowledge management, risk management, customer relationship management, enterprise resource planning, and business intelligence – to the detriment of innovative, strategic, big-picture visions.

Most businesses simply have no understanding of the bigger picture. While they're busy attending to the details, and wasting precious resources measuring goodness knows what, they lose the vision, the meaning and the appreciation of what is a rich and complex system of personal interactions. The business world excels at myopic thinking. And myopic thinking leads to dull, me-too mediocrity.

You call that choice?

The market provides an illusion of choice, but there's precious little real choice. Short-term MTV flicker-fashion means huge churn-over of goods, but offers no substantial differentiation. Waste for the sake of fleeting fashion is truly breathtaking. Walk into any major shopping centre today and you could be anywhere in the world – the sameness is totally demoralising. Centres are built to a rigid formula, which means less choice for consumers. Individuals are forced to go for "vintage" or "designer" offerings in a desperate attempt to avoid mediocrity.

Bottom-line birdcage

There's a serious lack of creativity. Organisations need to get some creative thinking and innovation happening if they want to be in the game for more than five minutes. Doing what everyone else is doing is an entry ticket only, and guess what? The ride 'aint gonna last very long! There's plenty of talk about nurturing talent and creativity, but what are organisations actually doing about it – seriously? You can learn about tools to enhance creativity, but you can't teach true creativity, and you certainly can't schedule it!

What they *can* do is provide a culture that embraces and stimulates talent, creative thinking and innovation, an environment that celebrates and rewards conceptual flexibility.

Innovation breakdown

What's desperately needed is a massive injection of innovation, enabling organisations to flourish, to stand out, and to create entirely new markets. Innovation arouses people's curiosity, and sings to the world that the company is interested in helping humankind to move forward, as opposed to just copying what everyone else is doing because it's what is selling today, never mind that it's taking us down a path of no return.

There's lots of talk about innovation, but little clarity, and certainly no clear consensus on where to get it. From an advertising agency? The marketing department? That funky design company next door? Do you have to hire weird people with red hair and piercings, and install a sushi bar where accounts receivable used to be, maybe?

Guess what? The source of innovation already resides within most organisations. They're called intrapreneurs!

Creative brain-drain

Many organisations already have just the talented, creative staff they need to provide the innovation they're desperate for, and who can make all the difference to their sustainability. These are the people who are constantly saying, 'There's a better way, there are other things we can do with this, other places we can take it.'

Unfortunately these people are hugely under-utilised, if not downright ignored, and sometimes even actively discouraged. They suggest ideas, but often get shouted down because of 'the way things have always been done around here.'

Little wonder intrapreneurs are irked by the seemingly entrenched mediocrity that surrounds them. Down with wasteful, boring business practices, and meaningless 'busyness'!

There's no doubt about it, intrapreneurs are out there, hidden within every organisation. The bad news is that some of the seriously creative types, the movers and shakers of the world, are being totally turned off business in its current state. Many are feeling stifled or drained by their employers, and are finding new ways to express their talents – going freelance, and/or becoming consultants, or branching out and re-emerging in completely different fields (e.g. the wellness industry) because they need an outlet for their intuition, creativity, and innate humanity.

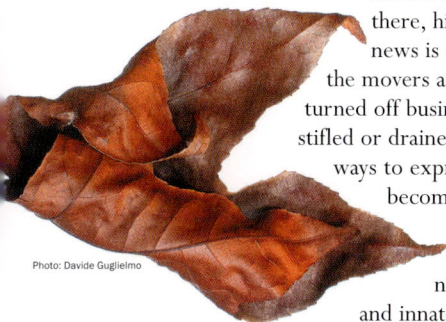

Photo: Davide Guglielmo

The X-chromosomes – they're out there somewhere!

The very male-dominated game that business has become, the "macho competition", is becoming increasingly boring. This could be one reason why women are becoming less and less attracted to conventional business, preferring instead to go it alone. Research indicates that women now run one third of Australia's small businesses, and in recent years there's been a significant increase in the number of businesses operated by women relative to men.

In a world where product features and quality are increasingly being trumped by genuine and engaging service as a point of difference, authentic communication, empathy, and relationship-building are the new crucial requirements for success. As Tom Peters has pointed out, women tend to be better at these things than men.

The feminine side within all of us represents an amazing potential source of competitive advantage. This is the part of us that deals predominantly with emotions, creativity, nurturing, relationship-building, empathy and kindness. Tapping into these skills opens up a whole new world of richer engagement with others. It helps us be more real. We need to change the macho game of business to one that is more embracing of whole selves. Just think what that would do for business, and the world!

Photo: Zern Liew

This book is for you, the intrapreneur

If you're looking for more than a desk, a job description and a regular payslip, this book will show you how to work successfully within the constraints of the corporate system, and unleash all the passion, energy and brilliant ideas that are bursting to find a means of expression.

Through years of our own personal frustration, and the frustration of our peers, friends, clients and colleagues, we've discovered some of the secrets to creating change. We're here to shake things up a bit – well, more than a bit, actually. We invite you to share in our knowledge and spread the word!

This book is a guide to unleashing your talents, fighting mediocrity, and helping you to get your ideas and innovations onto the agenda and out into the world without going insane in the process.

It will also help you to identify and work effectively with fellow innovators in the organisation to make exciting things happen.

We expose the flawed conventional thinking that has led the masses to the current state of mediocrity, and give you the tools needed to counter the pressure to think conventionally.

Applying the ideas and strategies presented in this book will enable you to throw off the shackles, explode out of the box, and initiate life-changing innovations in your work environment.

This is for the special people in organisations who burn with a genuine desire to be more innovative. So are you really an intrapreneur? Turn to the quiz in Chapter 1 and find out!

Photo: Zern Liew

Be part of the revolution

We're on the cusp of something exciting, and you're hereby invited to be a part of it. Our role is to empower you to apply your unique strengths and talents for positive change.

We're about helping rebel insurgents like you gain a stronger foothold in the beige boardrooms of carbon-copy corporations.

We need more innovation within organisations. A new mindset. A different way of doing things, not more of the same, regurgitated mindlessly through layers of sycophantic bureaucracy.

Organisations need to recognise the importance of attracting and actively nurturing intrapreneurs to initiate and drive innovation and change. In the meantime, you can start showing them the way by being the best intrapreneur that you can be.

Intrapreneurs know what they stand for. They just need a tipping point – which is what this book is.

We're excited, and you should be too!

Let the revolution begin!

The hungry spirit is a rebel with a cause!

Photo: Dain Hubley

1. Hello intrapreneurs!

Source photo: Jan De Bondt

Many extraordinary and world-changing business opportunities have been created by entrepreneurs who've refused to accept things as set-in-stone, have constantly asked why, and have seen much better alternatives to the established way of doing things. To change the game from inside the tent, we look to intrapreneurs like you.

The term intrapreneur was coined by Gifford Pinchot back in the 1980s .Whilst it has been in existence for some time, little has been done to date about recognising and assisting this creative group – and certainly to our knowledge no business book has come out of Australia on the topic.

What exactly is an intrapreneur?

An intrapreneur has the same traits as an entrepreneur – passion, creativity, and the conviction and desire to make a difference. They generally possess a healthy work ethic, a desire to excel at what they do, and an optimistic attitude towards obstacles.

Intrapreneurs are entrepreneurs by nature, working within the corporation. You are those passionate, intelligent, highly creative, but often constrained and frustrated rebels that lurk within all organisations. You are the courageous and authentic questioning minds, the tireless seekers of "a better way".

It's definitely possible to work within corporations AND be innovative. You don't have to leave and start your own business, or wait until you make CEO. Innovation can happen right now.

Intrapreneurs like you want to see the organisations you work for flourish, and achieve greatness. You want your organisation to help make the world a better place.

Intrapreneurs derive intrinsic meaning from their work. That's why, most of all, you want to find an outlet for all your amazing ideas, and see them take flight.

Given the right environment, with support, guidance, and freedom to experiment and make mistakes, intrapreneurs can make powerful contributions way beyond the benefits of any short-term cost-cutting exercises recommended by expensive management consultants.

The joy of intrapreneuring

Intrapreneuring is a way to claim ownership of, and express, your true self and core values, a way to obtain intrinsic satisfaction within the organisation in which you work.

It's about finding all the opportunities for creativity, innovation and freshness that you crave – without having to leave your job.

Intrapreneurs constantly seek out opportunities to create value. In many ways, they think and operate as though they were an independent enterprise within their organisation – intrapreneurs run intraprises!

As an intrapreneur, it's up to *you* to seize the moment and start something extraordinary within your organisation. If not you,

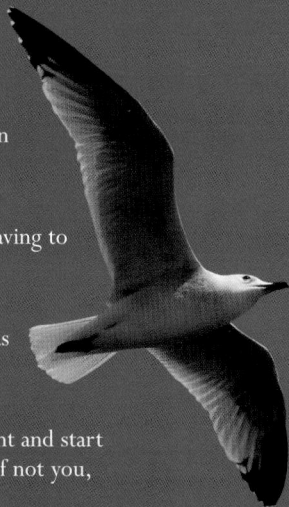

then who else? You're the first and last chance for creative thinking and innovation. One thing's for sure – you can't sit around waiting for something or someone else to fix it. It ain't gonna happen!

It's imperative that you care passionately, and that you're prepared to stand up and be counted. This is for your life, for the lives of your children, and for the future of the world. This is serious!

"It's not the big companies that eat the small; it's the fast that eat the slow."

Wall Street Journal

You are not alone!

You probably feel like it's you against the whole world sometimes, but take heart – there are other people within your organisation who are feeling exactly the same way about things.

Go forth and find them. You'll benefit from meeting each other, sharing your creative thinking and optimistic attitude, helping each other to galvanise your collective thoughts, and spurring you into action.

Successful intrapreneuring is definitely a team sport! There will be people within your own organisation who would love to work with you to make extraordinary things happen. This is about finding people of like-mind to start a revolution.

Are you an intrapreneur?

Take the quiz on the next page and find out if you're really an intrapreneur!

Photo: Dez Pain

The Intrapreneurs Quiz

How much do you agree with the following statements? If you strongly disagree, give yourself a score of 0. If you strongly agree, give yourself a score of 2. If you sort of agree, give yourself a score of 1. When you've finished, add up your score, and check the guide at the end of the quiz to find out how intrapreneurial you really are!

I know who I am, what my values and beliefs are, and what I stand for.	0	1	2
I act with integrity towards myself. My actions usually truthfully reflect who I am.	0	1	2
People who know me can identify my work or my influence on a project just by experiencing that project.	0	1	2
I have an identifiable personal 'brand' that is aligned with who I am.	0	1	2
I love conversations that start with "I have this idea...". I have lots of ideas.	0	1	2
I am curious about many different things. I know lots of weird stuff.	0	1	2
I know a diverse range of people with different backgrounds, lifestyles, education and vocations.	0	1	2
I can see patterns in how things work, and how people engage with each other.	0	1	2
When faced with rules, I enjoy understanding the reasons behind them, and thinking of ways to get around them.	0	1	2
When faced with a challenge, I am more often excited by the possibilities than the scary bits.	0	1	2
I love getting behind a worthy cause.	0	1	2
When I tell people about my passions, they usually get excited with it as well.	0	1	2

I want to make a difference in the world. ⓪ ① ②

If I believe in something strongly, I will stand up for it. ⓪ ① ②

I love challenging convention. I enjoy pushing against the envelope. ⓪ ① ②

The phrase 'taking risks' primarily says adventure and excitement to me. ⓪ ① ②

When I make a mistake, I am willing to own up and take responsibility for it. ⓪ ① ②

I enjoy working within the system to make changes. I like the idea of being the rebel inside the ranks. ⓪ ① ②

Rules and constraints are there to be worked around. ⓪ ① ②

Bureaucracy and systems are not 'bad', they are only means to ends. ⓪ ① ②

I enjoy looking at the bigger picture. I try to do this even when the immediate task does not require it. ⓪ ① ②

I am conscious that my actions have wider repercussions for others, and for my community. ⓪ ① ②

I think of myself as an integral part of a larger system called Life. ⓪ ① ②

I love dreaming up new and fantastic visions of what could be. ⓪ ① ②

I enjoy thinking about lots of different things. Especially how some of my visions could become reality. ⓪ ① ②

I enjoy rolling up my sleeves and getting into the action. ⓪ ① ②

I like making stuff happen as much as I like thinking up new ideas. (0)(1)(2)

I am generally an optimistic person. (0)(1)(2)

There are things I am very passionate about. I get butterflies in my stomach. (0)(1)(2)

I am quite aware of my emotional state. (0)(1)(2)

When I am not feeling that good, I am kind to myself, and allow myself time to work through the negative feelings. (0)(1)(2)

I enjoy engaging and working with like-minded people. (0)(1)(2)

I am good at working with others. People generally feel comfortable around me. (0)(1)(2)

I am aware of, and take responsibility for, the impact of my actions on others. (0)(1)(2)

I am accepting of differences in others. (0)(1)(2)

Success to me is always more than just the money. (0)(1)(2)

When looking for a job, I tend to get more excited about the type of work on offer than the pay. (0)(1)(2)

I am comfortable saying "I don't know". (0)(1)(2)

I would rather be known for doing a great job than for making a lot of money. (0)(1)(2)

I volunteer my time and skills for community causes. (0)(1)(2)

How did you do?

If you scored 60-80: You are most definitely an intrapreneur. You're ready to take on the world!

If you scored 30-59: Your inner intrapreneur is starting to show through. Feed and nourish it by reading the rest of this book!

If you scored 0-29: Hmmm... either someone tied you down and forced you to read this book OR hiding in there somewhere is a mini-intrapreneur that wants the real you to come out... but it's going to take a LOT of work. Read this book, absorb everything like a sponge, and practice everything that we suggest. Oh and throw out anything that remotely looks like something Gary would wear or do - in fact do the opposite!

Can you identify with the mindset of an intrapreneur? If you're feeling a little unsure about one or more aspects, here's the good news. The answers lie within you. There's no need to despair, no need to start looking for remedial courses at your local college. It's all in the mind.

Attitude rules!

> *"Life is either a daring adventure or nothing."*
>
> Helen Keller

Photo: Rachel Fuller

This is Gary.
Gary is our anti-intrapreneur.

In a nutshell, intrapreneurs are:

Long-term thinkers
not fulfilment of immediate needs and instant gratification

Wide, encompassing, inclusive, flexible thinkers
not the narrow black/white inflexible view

Aware their actions affect a lot of people
not actions serving only to meet one's personal requirements

Empowered
not victims

Movers and shakers
not followers and spectators

Self-aware, responsible, lifelong learners
not blamers and avoiders

"How Can We Help" people
not "What's In It For Me?" people

Photo: Jean Scheijen

Intrapreneurs tend to have a brand of their own without even trying!
A brand is a consistent articulation of an integrated personality – a
person's values, dreams, skills, and integrity. You can often sense
an intrapreneur's brand from what they do, because they're so true
to who they are!

**Intrapreneurs want to do it for themselves,
but also for the organisation they work for!**

Innovation is about:

1. **Business** – Creation and exchange of real value. Meaningful work. Work to enable and enrich whole lives. Grassroots agility. Authenticity. Alignment with values.

2. **Design** – Imagination. Curiosity. Understanding. Elucidation. Creation. Using design thinking as a critical and rigorous business problem-solving tool. Create possibilities.

3. **Reality** – Embracing and leveraging real-world constraints. Usable and appropriate business outcomes. Dream, then make very real!

4. **Community** – Making a difference. The spirit of abundance. Sharing and giving as a fundamentally rich, rewarding and creative experience.

5. **Collaboration** – Connection with others. Wide-ranging dialogue and story-telling. Partnering on diverse, worthwhile and fun projects. Togetherness.

6. **Truth** – Working and living truthfully to who you are. Bringing your whole self to your work. Talking your talk and walking your walk.

7. **People** – Respect, openess and kindness. Engage with others' passions and dreams. Enable others. Positive, empowering, respectful outcomes.

Zern Liew • www.eicolab.com

▪ What is innovation anyway?

Invention

A never-before seen, brand new concept. Usually the product of scientific R&D or serious thinking.

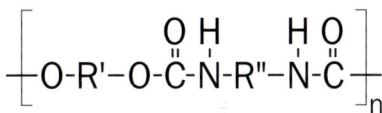

$$\left[\begin{array}{c} \quad\quad O\;H\quad\quad\;\;H\;O \\ \mid\quad\quad\;\| \;\mid \quad\quad\quad\;\mid\; \| \\ O\text{-}R'\text{-}O\text{-}C\text{-}N\text{-}R''\text{-}N\text{-}C \end{array} \right]_n$$

Innovation

A new invention or a combination of existing concepts made emotionally desirable and therefore commercially viable.

Improvement

A change that has minor impact on the fundamental nature of the underlying concept; but serves to extend the emotional appeal and on-going (usually short term) commercial viability.

Photos: Zern Liew

Invention: polyurethane foam. Innovation: a stress ball. Improvement: multicoloured stress balls.

2. Attitude

David Egan *Original Sin*, 2002,
178 x 128cm, acrylic on canvas

Egan Gallery
3a Glenmore Rd Paddington NSW
www.egangallery.com

"How do you teach obsession?"

Anita Roddick

Isn't innovation something you can learn? It's a bunch of creative thinking tools, right? Or is it what they do over at the ad agency? Aren't the guys down in the marketing department on it already?

You can't be trained to be innovative. Nor can you be trained to be an intrapreneur. You can't go to a three-day power course and come out all innovative. You can certainly be aware of the traits of those who innovate, but that's about it. Many companies think that teaching their staff the best or trendiest creativity tools will suddenly make them innovative, only to end up sorely disappointed.

Certificate of Innovation

Presented to:

for having successfully learnt all the currently available creativity and thinking tools on this planet.

(Incidentally, loads of free creativity tools can be had on: www.innovationtools.com)

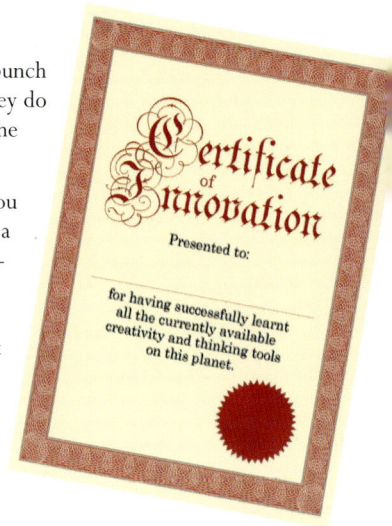

Why attitude?

Want to be truly innovative? It all starts with your attitude.

The innovator's attitude is the sum total of your values, beliefs and dreams, your perceptions of yourself and others and the world, the way you treat yourself and others, and the way you think about and approach life.

Tools like De Bono's hats, bubble diagrams and concept fans can and should be learnt, but they're no substitute for the right attitude. If your attitude is wrong, these tools will only give you a false sense of security. Going through the motions of applying creativity and thinking tools without an innovative attitude will not make you innovative.

If you don't have the underlying attitude to be innovative, no amount of creativity tools and techniques will turn you into an intrapreneur. These tools and techniques need a solid foundational attitude to work from.

However if you don't already have the attitude for innovation, you *can* do something about it. You can choose to start cultivating the attitude for innovation right now. Stop saying 'I'll do this when …'. The time for action is now. Life's too short to live uncreatively!

The next segment talks about how you can develop the attitudinal traits of intrapreneurs. We look at each of the traits of an intrapreneur (from the quiz) and present some ideas on how to develop them.

If you've already got the attitude thing happening, feel free to skip straight to the next chapter!

Who are you?
If you want to be someone – be yourself!

Getting the attitude

Dare to be yourself

In today's high speed, multimedia, multitasking world, many of us develop fractured personas. We're one person at work, a different person at home, and yet another person when socialising with our friends.

So how do you find your true self? How do you find your life's purpose?

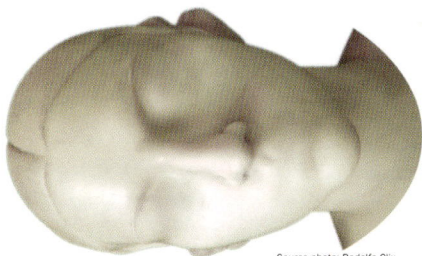
Source photo: Rodolfo Clix

You need to be connected with your truth, living and breathing it every day. People often say that they're ready for action, if only they could figure out exactly what it is that they want to achieve. The fact that we're often distracted by other people's expectations – what they want from us, or want us to be – doesn't help.

Understand that you're only accountable to yourself, and responsible for how you perceive the world. You can't control how others perceive you, although you can control how you present your true self to them.

Being true to yourself frees you to engage with the challenges of the world! Instead of spending all your energies maintaining different and often shifting personas, you gain a solid immutable core of who you are, and can focus all your energy on engaging authentically with the outside world.

Being true to yourself also helps your decision-making. Are you choosing a career for yourself, or for someone else? Are you living life in terms of your own expectations, or in terms of someone else's?

Get into ideas

If you're not an inherently curious person, it's possible to develop your powers of curiosity through practise. Start with your passions. Choose one, for example Indian cuisine, and commit to delving into it as deeply as possible. Determine to find out everything you can about every facet of it, all the herbs and spices, where they come from, how they're prepared, recipes, regional differences, how food impacts on Indian culture, history and society, and so on.

Be curious – about everything!

Now start branching out sideways. Select a specific area of interest, for example the herbs and spices. Now go deeper, and list all the related aspects. Discover what species they belong to, where they originated, who the chief producers are around the world, and how to grow them. Then branch off again. Choose a country that produces one particular spice, say cumin, as a starting point. Resolve to learn something about the country that's totally unrelated to food.

Photo: Paolo Ferla

As you've probably already realised, the internet is an ideal tool for this type of exploration. So yes, we encourage you to spend some time surfing the net – with a passionate purpose!

Intrapreneurs are inherently curious by nature. They have an insatiable desire to learn about anything and everything, and an open mind that leads them to think and play beyond narrow traditional frameworks. They love having fun, and refuse to take things too seriously. They're absolutely comfortable with 'I don't know', and are constantly asking "Why?", "Why not?" and "How?"

The more you develop your curiosity, the more you open yourself up to new possibilities and new life-paths. This makes you an invaluable problem-solving and option-spotting guru. The more disparate knowledge you can draw on, the more raw ingredients you have with which to free-associate. This is what enables you to be truly creative and innovative!

Why?
Why not?
How?

Meet Trinity, our model intrapreneur.

Find a cause that moves you

Intrapreneurs have a burning need to make a difference. They focus on producing extraordinary results. For them, it's not just about making money. They have a passion for producing something enduring and meaningful. A neat way to think about this is in terms of a cause.

A cause is something that inspires you to get out there and do something. On bad days, a cause keeps you going. A cause guides your actions at all times, and feeds the part of you that needs meaningful direction. Talk to any intrapreneur and they'll tell you that they have a burning desire to leave their footprints on the world. They pursue causes that resonate with their values and personalities, and constantly inspire and drive their creative energy.

Finding what moves you requires some time for reflection. Think about the last time you felt really good. What did you do that evoked those feelings? What were the tangible and emotional outcomes? In what way did you make a difference?

Beware the distraction of great opportunities.

Sometimes, you are presented with what appears to be a great opportunity, one that connects with your passions, speaks of adventure, and suits your skill-set perfectly. But it is a total distraction! This is when you connect back to your cause. Does the amazing opportunity serve your cause?

Beware of focusing excessively on technical or logistical achievements. Try to delve into the deeper emotional rewards. Was winning that web design award really what did it for you? Or was it the sense of empowering a client towards realising his or her dreams?

Take a risk

Intrapreneurs have the inner strength necessary to take on a challenge, and the persistence to stick at it. Such strength and tenacity is critical if you want to make a real difference. You can't change the world while you're hiding under your doona.

What are you afraid of? What is the worst that can happen? Would you care in 6 months time?

If you're somewhat addicted to comfort (and we know how tempting it can be), try this exercise: Conduct little experiments every day that force you to take yourself at least a small way out of your comfort zone. This could be tasting a new cuisine, or talking to a stranger on the train. Discover that the world doesn't end when you stretch yourself! Gradually increase the scariness of the scenarios until you become more comfortable operating beyond your comfort zone. Congratulations! You've already become a much braver commando!

Intrapreneurs have a strong sense of adventure. They know what fear smells like, but take a deep breath and do it anyway. Taking a risk is never easy, but half the fun is

Think as big as you can and go for it!

the mingling sense of fear and exhilaration just before you take the plunge!

It might be the hardest thing you've ever done, but you need to acknowledge your fears, challenge them, and at least control, if not conquer, them. Only then will you be free to live your life to the max, and guess what? The sense of achievement is indescribable!

Embrace constraints and reality

"Get real!" Do people say this to you occasionally? Whatever their intentions, we recommend that you choose to interpret it as a kind and gentle reminder to take a reality check.

Embracing reality is an important intrapreneurial trait because, for better or worse, we all have to live and work in the real world. Ideas, dreams and visions are important starting points in your quest to change the world. But for innovation to actually happen, you need to take action. And to be truly effective, you need to work within the constraints of the world as we know it. Operating in a parallel universe is not part of the game!

Working with constraints means compromise. For intrapreneurs, the question is almost always how much to compromise, and when; it's rarely how to avoid compromise altogether. Learning to accept and work with (or around!) obstacles will make your intrapreneuring life much easier, and at the same time, much more interesting.

Embracing reality provides another advantage. Identifying where the boundaries are at the start of your project can help reduce the variables, and serve to shortlist the options for the way forward. Of course the caveat is that you need to know the difference between genuine constraints you need to work with or around, constraints that are real but can be challenged, and red-herring constraints, such as your self-limiting beliefs, that need to be stared down!

Working within the bounds of reality also enables other people to more easily understand and buy into your cause and your project. It makes it easier for you to create a fan club!

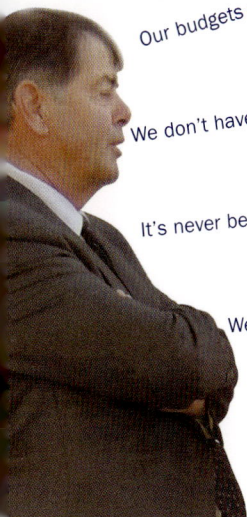

Our budgets are too tight.

Let's be creative. Can we take funds out of stationery?

We don't have enough staff.

Let's attract some freelancers or volunteers.

It's never been done this way before.

This is a fantastic opportunity to be the leader.

We don't have the distribution channels.

We'll form strategic alliances – with our competitors.

Photo: Rachel Fuller

There are loads of opportunities to connect with the present. Turn off that iPod! Next time you're in a taxi, ask the driver for her opinion on something. Next time you're on a train, listen in to the conversations around you.

Next time you stop and play with your pet, be 100% present in the moment, and stop worrying about the future or revisiting the past. Lessons are everywhere!

Big picture outlook

In today's world, both the education system and the corporate world actively encourage specialisation and reductionist thinking. We're trained to think and work within a narrowly-defined field – be this accounting, waste management, or faciomaxillary surgery.

This limiting approach to thinking, learning and work poses a significant threat to our ongoing ability to foster innovation. The more we focus on 'our jobs' and 'our specialty', the less we know (or have time to know) about what else is out there in the world. The less of the big picture we can see, the more stifled we become and the less we're able to be creative and innovative, because creativity is about seeing the unexpected, and linking seemingly unrelated concepts.

Learning to see the big picture requires a change of mindset. You can still work within your specialty of course, but start to observe the world around you with active curiosity. Stand up right now and take a look beyond your cubicle walls –

what do you see? What's new and different? List five
things you can see that are totally unrelated to your
specialty. Now jump on to the Internet and find out
as much as you can about them!

Look at the media you consume. Try buying
different magazines, and switching to TV channels
you don't normally watch. Start cultivating new
friends who don't live around the corner, or work
in a related field. Take up new hobbies, dabble in an
evening course in something completely unrelated
to your everyday life. Try anything once!

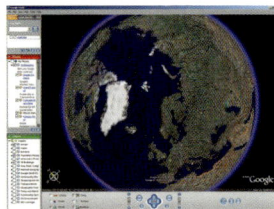

A cool way to practise a big
picture view is Google Earth.
Download it and see the world
from a whole new perspective.
http://earth.google.com

Dreamer, thinker and doer in one

The unique talent of an intrapreneur lies in his/
her ability to see the big picture, dream big
dreams, develop exciting plans, galvanise others
into action, and turn those dreams into reality.

If you need to work on dreaming: Revisit
your childhood dreams. Perhaps even revisit the

**How strong are you in each of
these areas: Dream; Think; Do?
Rate yourself 1-5 against each
one. Which areas do you need
to work on?**

place where you grew up, to help spark your memories. Indulge in fantasies
(they're your very own fantasies, so yes, anything goes!). Look around your world.
What pisses you off? What gives you immense joy? What could be better about
your life, your work or your project? What do you really want to be doing? Ask
'What if?' and 'What could be?'

Dreaming is blue-sky fun – mundane, everyday reality is not permitted! The only
judgement call you're allowed to make is whether a dream truly, deeply excites
and moves you. Dream of positives – of magical, exciting, wondrous possibilities.
This is not an exercise in finding things to be bitter about!

If you need to work on thinking: This is where you take a dream and make it
fit within the bounds of reality as bravely as you can. List all the constraints that
you think will limit your dream. Now list all the assets that you think will help you
make your dream come true.

Go for a walk, grab a coffee, and re-examine these lists. How many of the constraints are real? How many of them can be challenged? How many are false
constraints?

Many people mistakenly believe that thinking is something that you do solely inside
your head. They also think that it's a skill that is innate within us all. As with any

other skill, you need to commit time and effort to learning and practising thinking. We like writing lists, talking to our friends over coffee, drawing bubble diagrams, or just plain doodling.

Just as a photographer carries a camera around to capture any opportunities that appear unexpectedly, as a practicing thinker you need to carry a notebook and pen around with you, or maybe a digital recorder. Use these to help you capture any sudden and interesting ideas, or to help you to set out and organise your thoughts.

Thinking is as concrete, enjoyable and rewarding as it gets. Think about it!

CapMaps are Creative, Analytical and Practical Visual Note-Taking Maps that incorporate many kinds of visual learning techniques to help information stand-out and excite the brain.

Visual learning techniques include – writing words in a creative way, converting words into pictures & symbols, using visual design elements such as chunks, patterns and mind-maps. The CapMap involves many learning styles and gives people the essence of the information in a creative and memorable way.

To learn more about CapMaps go to www.glenncapelli.com where educator and creator of CapMaps, Glenn Capelli provides further information and resources on a whole range of creative learning and memory techniques.

If you need to work on doing: Be open to doing something at least once. Strive to move beyond a "this is not my job" mindset.

If fear is holding you back, know that it's okay not to know, and to make mistakes. There's always someone to ask for help. And you never know, reaching out for help could lead to some exciting new collaborations, or inspire a whole new wave of innovative thinking.

Maybe the scale of the whole thing is proving a little daunting. Remember how you eat an elephant – one bite at a time. So what are you waiting for? You do know how to use a knife and fork don't you? Bon appetit!

Whether you believe something is possible or not, either way, you're right!

Passion and optimism

Intrapreneurs are optimists. They focus on what is possible. Mistakes and failures are sources of learning, and the means to new paths for our journey.

Optimism can be learned! It's simply a matter of shifting your perceptions. You can choose to be optimistic.

This doesn't mean you go into denial mode and bury any negative emotions that appear, as they do, from time to time. You need to acknowledge these, embrace them, and explore them. The challenge is to keep them in perspective. When things go wrong, or we make a mistake, or we don't get what we desire, it's totally okay to feel sad, hurt and disappointed. An optimist doesn't try to bury these feelings, nor does he/she let them assume an unreasonable and ultimately debilitating prominence.

The Freedom of Choice means you can always choose to see things differently.

Learning to be an optimist takes practise. When an unfavourable situation arises, acknowledge your negative emotions. Write them down in great detail – this is enormously helpful. Give yourself a reasonable amount of time to sit with, and work through, these emotions. Be gentle on yourself. Then think about the positives that could arise from the situation. Write these down as well. Maybe you'll even begin to see the funny side of things!

Engage authentically with people

Intrapreneuring is a team sport. Building strong, cohesive teams requires you to connect with people in a genuine way. To relate positively to people, and to engage them in your cause, requires authenticity. This in turn requires self-awareness, and empowered, considered decision-making. It's about taking responsibility for being true to your authentic self.

It's vital that intrapreneurs have high emotional intelligence. You need to be comfortable working with your emotions. How else can you learn to listen for, and trust implicitly, the all-important gut-feelings and intuition that reside within us all? Have you ever disregarded your warning feelings and caved in to logic or external pressure, only to discover that you should have been true to your inner sage?

There are five aspects to emotional intelligence: self-awareness, self-management, self-motivation, empathy and compassion, and the ability to handle relationships.

The first three aspects involve the self, while the other two are about how we relate to others.

Intrapreneurs need a high degree of self-awareness, self-management and motivation. You need to be able to reflect on your thoughts and actions, and to see, understand, and accept your whole self in order to know, and act in ways that honour, your driving personal cause.

A lack of emotional intelligence is a dangerous thing. It can destroy teams, and despite the best of intentions, turn potential allies into arch enemies.

At the end of the day, intrapreneuring is about people, ideas and emotions. It's about engaging people to embrace your ideas and values. Creative, analytical and practical, intelligence sure helps, but it is emotional intelligence that enables the possibility of AND.

Reminder: Be kind to yourself. Intrapreneurs can often be very demanding and harsh on themselves. Think of it this way – if it was a good friend going through the same situation instead of you, would your expectations be kinder? Apply this kindness to yourself!

If not now, when?

You don't need permission, more experience, or a bunch of fancy qualifications. You don't need to be a techno-geek, you don't need money, and you don't need an invitation.

So, are you ready?

Awareness! Empowerment! Change! It all starts from within. Do you know what you stand for?

"Be where you are or you will miss your life"

Buddha

"Whatever you can do or dream, begin it. Boldness has genius, magic and power in it. Begin it now."

Goethe

Photo: Jin Neoh

Tourism Australia

Andrew McEvoy, Director, Organisational Development

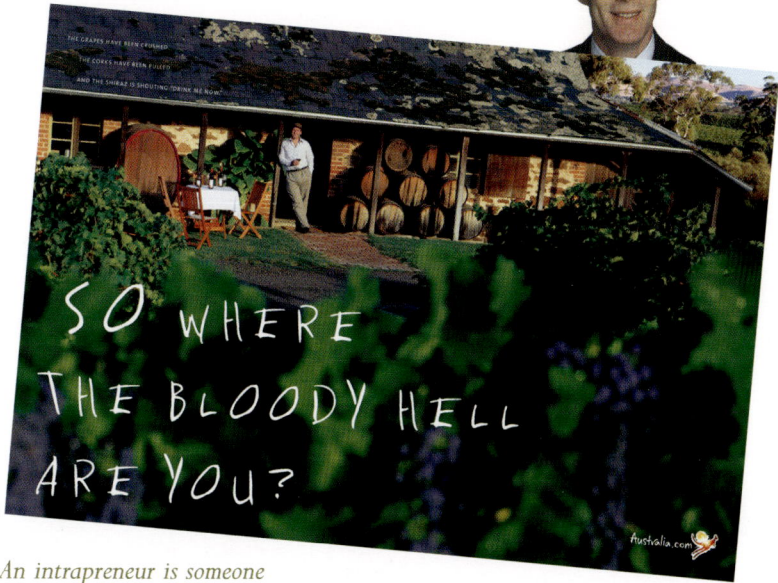

THE GRAPES HAVE BEEN CRUSHED
THE CORKS HAVE BEEN PULLED
AND THE SHIRAZ IS SHOUTING 'DRINK ME NOW'

SO WHERE THE BLOODY HELL ARE YOU?

australia.com

An intrapreneur is someone who helps shape an organisation and meet challenges in innovative ways. They don't have to be senior executives – just people who take an alternate view of how to get things done, and have a track record of success through taking this approach.

I think Australians have had to be innovative over the years to meet the challenges of distinctly Australian conditions. Through technology, we are now much closer to the world than ever before, but throughout our history we have had to deal with time and distance and this has made us clever, resilient and determined.

Intrapreneurs need to be heard, to keep them satisfied and ensure that they don't leave. Hierarchical organisations struggle to let their intrapreneurs out of the cage. A culture that encourages people to challenge the norm is essential. The Gen Xers amongst us are also looking to be rewarded for ideas, innovation, problem-solving and success, so these things need to be acknowledged.

47

Work should include some good old fashioned fun. Personally, I've always thrived in an environment which encouraged success. It's something I very much respect about the American culture.

Tourism Australia is constantly looking to improve the ways in which we encourage creativity, innovation and individualism.

We try to work in cross-functional groups to get the best out of people's problem-solving abilities. We certainly celebrate success, and make a point of highlighting the role played by individuals. You should never be afraid to name names where appropriate.

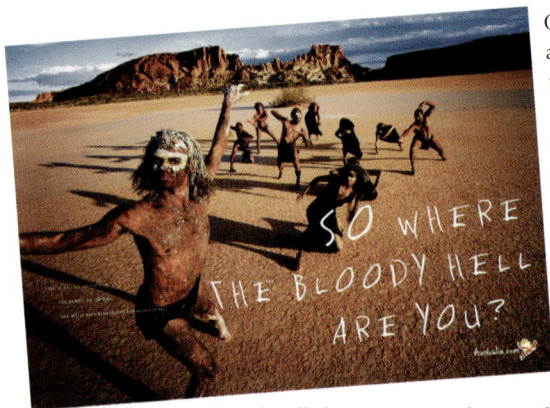

Our physical environment is also very open and looks out on the world – as indeed we should. Finally, we try to bring the client, stakeholder or consumer into our meetings and conversations. Instead of disappearing in a haze of constant internal thinking, we try to get an outside view.

A recent innovation has been rewarding employees who take all their recreation leave. Like all Australian companies it seems, we have an issue with getting people to take the annual leave that is due to them. Australian businesses have accrued more than 70 million days (which means more than $11 billion in wages) that, in terms of our vision, we would like to see used to stimulate domestic tourism.

In attempting to address this issue, Tourism Australia has instituted a program called No Leave, No Life, aimed at encouraging employees to take their annual leave when it is due.

Tourism Australia is leading the charge by rewarding all staff who take their full entitlement in a 12 month period with an extra three days holidays! People love it. They strive to qualify for the bonus so they can celebrate with more Aussie holidays.

People have come to expect a humanised workplace. In a time of low unemployment, the labour market is very competitive. If you want great people, they'd better like coming to work. That applies across all generations, but is a particularly defining factor for the Gen Y workforce.

Companies that ignore their staff and think new ideas can only come from external sources do so at their peril.

Many organisations apply too much focus on the bottom line and not enough on creativity. Tourism Australia takes our role as a leverage marketing organisation extremely seriously. And to do that people have to have fun. The global consumer wants to come to a destination they will enjoy, so we had better be able to communicate that. Tourism Australia is perceived externally as being a very creative and fun brand.

We give out "Shine" awards, which are gift vouchers, to people who live the values of fun and commitment to innovation.

We don't encourage people to become mavericks – that's going too far. Mavericks tend to cut corners and take on too much risk, and end up on wanted posters with a bounty on their head. In fact, we've tightened up our processes, systems and risk profile in recent times. The best organisations are those that inspire creativity within a tighter framework.

In order to get their ideas heard, rather than being squashed by bureaucracy, intrapreneurs need to work within their circle of influence. The determined intrapreneur will be heard!

None of us stays with one organisation forever these days. This means that while we're there, we need to work towards leaving a legacy. Most people want to see the organisation they work for be successful, and to do that you need to breed the next generation of ideas and innovations. The only way to do that is to support and encourage people.

Eager young intrapreneurs should always maintain respect for those who have gone before them. Longevity breeds experience, and respect for this can prove very helpful. Ultimately, you have to be true to your drive and ideas, but if you figure out how to go about this with tact and respect, you will prevail.

The one big thing that makes Tourism Australia stand out in terms of encouraging and nurturing creativity and innovative thinking is the feeling that what you're doing makes a real difference for Australia – from global perceptions to economic performance, and the creation of jobs for ourselves and our kids. It's almost like a cause. If this is the feeling, you can't help but be creative and innovative.

www.australia.com

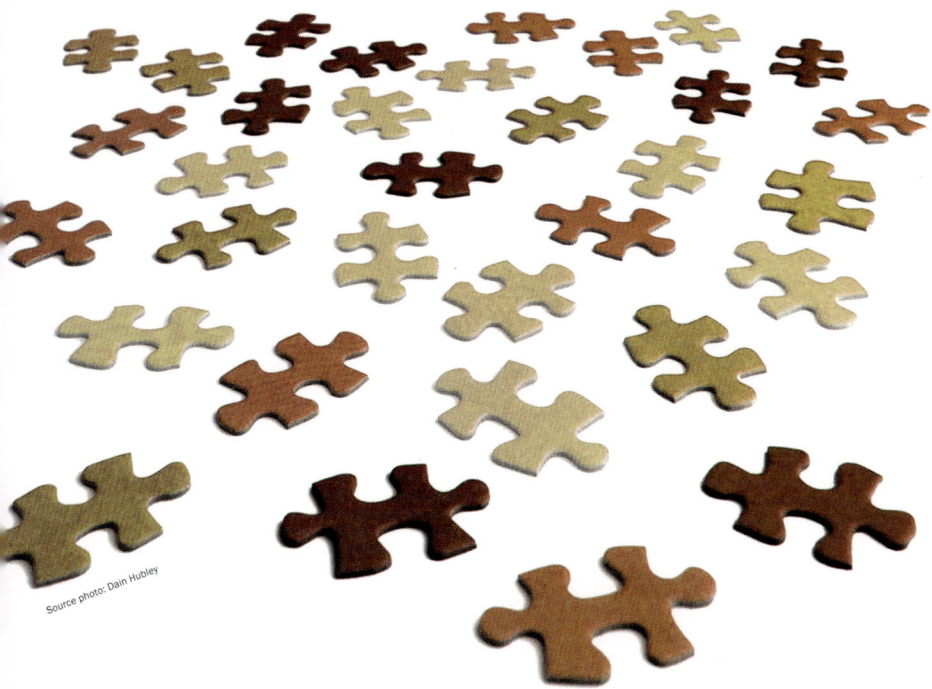

3. People

It's all about you – not!

Let's get one thing clear – if you want great things to happen, you need to work with people. It's not just about you, the intrapreneur.

Until now, you've probably found yourself working with a random bunch of people. If you've been fortunate, things have gone swimmingly. Chances are though, you've probably found the experience underwhelming. It's hard to work with people who don't believe in what they're doing, or who aren't working towards a greater cause.

It's vitally important to recognise the power of working with others. There's only so much one person can do, no matter how passionate you are. The good news is, you don't have to do it all by yourself. Fellow travelling companions are out there. Great businesses are built by teams – inspired and led by intrapreneurs, of course.

So who are the right people? Most people can be the right people, when they're treated the right way! Most people have the potential to commit to and strive for excellence – if only they can be inspired. The trick lies in converting long-ignored and un-appreciated colleagues into true believers in your cause to change the world.

It's often tempting for intrapreneurs to chuck it all in and go solo when things aren't going well, and all you can see is obstacles. Before you do anything hasty, step back and explore the option of staying within the organisation and making a real difference with the resources at your fingertips

Intrapreneurs and managers

Intrapreneurs can come in all shapes and sizes – even managers. All too often we think of intrapreneurs as the rule-breaking, maverick, new-hire employee. We've got news for you – established managers can be intrapreneurial as well. The new-hire may not know the rules, and may use this to their advantage, but on the other hand, the established manager has the 'know the rules well enough to know what can be broken' card to play. It's not so much about the position in which you find yourself in the corporate hierarchy as it is about your attitude.

From our observations over the years, most managers tend to be stewards, people who, along with bean counters and passive investors are, by nature, not renowned for their innovative tendencies. They often seek to limit change (i.e. innovation), with a view to maximising short-term returns and minimising risk. Their focus on fast money and change avoidance can result in a loss of direction and momentum, with serious consequences. When intrapreneurs cede power to steward-managers, organisations risk losing their innovative heart and soul.

Intrapreneurs need the opportunity to influence the strategic direction of the business at all levels. If you're an intrapreneurial manager, you're in a very enviable position. Leverage it well. If you're not a manager, start cultivating your manager, and explore different ways to get ideas on the table and exciting things happening.

Ideally, organisations need to create a culture where intrapreneurs are encouraged to operate as the CEOs of their own intraprises within the organisation. This means giving intrapreneurs the authority and resources to initiate and execute their own projects. And the permission to engage the hearts and minds of their colleagues.

Hiring an intrapreneurial CEO is not a real fix for a fundamentally un-innovative organisation.

Encouraging intrapreneurs to be the CEOs of their own intraprises within the larger organisation is not necessarily a recipe for chaos and anarchy either. It's about achieving a balance between authority and freedom, between responsibility and accountability.

Assembling your dream team

As we mentioned earlier, intrapreneuring isn't a job for the lone ranger. As the CEO of your own intraprise, you need to reach out and gather a dream team to help execute your project.

So where do you find these people? Look around you! There are people around you now with huge amounts of untapped potential just waiting for someone like you to lead them out into the sunshine.

Start meeting them. Talk to them about what they do. Find out what moves them. What are they annoyed about at work? What are they really happy with? What do they get up to in their cubicles when no one's watching? What do they think about in the lift?

Tell them (enthusiastically of course) about your projects and ideas and thoughts. Look for people who operate on your wavelength. Watch for the sparkle in their eyes while they're listening to you, or while they're talking about something they care deeply about. Look for the intrapreneuring attitude. Buy them a copy of this book, and get them to do the quiz on Chapter 1!

Be the boss you wish you'd always had. Intrapreneurs need to become the manager they always wished they'd had. Most people (including intrapreneurs) desperately want a manager who listens and considers their input. Someone who makes them feel valued. You need to do the same for your team.

Beware of 'official' organisational charts. They totally fail to recognise the powerful network of informal relationships that invariably develop within organisations. What they do not show is how individuals actually relate to each other, and contribute to each other's productivity and wellbeing, irrespective of actual titles or positions in the hierarchy.

The elements of an effective team

Photo: Emin Ozkan

There are several fairly distinct roles in any successful project team. One person may fill more than one role. Indeed in some smaller projects, one person may be the whole team!

Which role are you playing now? Which roles have you played? How many of these roles can you play effectively at the same time? Are there any roles you prefer not to play?

Innovator

The innovator (that's you, the intrapreneur) is the ideas-engine behind the project. Without your attitude and ideas, the project would not have taken off in the first place. But the innovator has to be more than just an inventor. The innovator turns ideas into tangible outcomes.

The innovator imbues the project with passion, optimism, enthusiasm and zest. You're constantly generating new ideas, while inspiring others in your team to generate ideas of their own. You lead the creative problem-solving sorties.

Sometimes, the innovator may not hang around to see the initial idea through to fruition. Once the high-level strategies have been taken care of, and the project is underway, the innovator can be off looking for the next cool project to start on.

Some innovators may not have the necessary focus to manage the project through to completion, or to execute every detailed task. They tend to be more interested in the bigger picture.

Leader

The project leader is the person who keeps the team together, focused, and on-track towards achieving the project goals.

This person is likely to actually manage the project. He/she needs the ability to focus on details, while at the same time keeping a keen eye on the big picture goals and inspiring others to deliver what is required.

A leader needs a great deal of emotional intelligence, maturity, and an inclusive and tolerant attitude to enable them to work well with, and bring out the best in, a diverse range of personalities.

Photo: Zern Liew

Doer

He/she is the one who is focused on translating ideas into actions and outcomes.

Projects often feature multiple doers, including external suppliers. It's worth thinking about how you can encourage external suppliers to feel a part of your project team.

An ideal doer is someone who not only executes well, but has also fully bought in to the big picture. They may even suggest valuable practical improvements during the project as a result of emerging information or knowledge! You can actively encourage this by ensuring doers feel involved, that they're a vital part of the team, and that their contribution is valued.

Doers can sometimes become annoyed by the innovator's apparent 'lack of focus' and by frequent requests for changes and improvements. Doers are more concerned with locking down the specifications, and then working diligently towards meeting them.

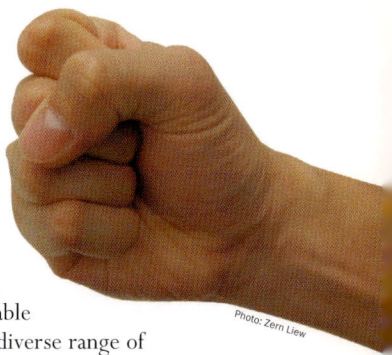

Evangelist

The evangelist is the one who sells the product or service to customers or stakeholders. He/she knows the target audience well, is always listening to customers, and is responsive to their needs. The evangelist knows how to present the product or service to the target audience in ways that address their particular needs. He/she is constantly working to build positive relationships.

Photo: Davide Guglielmo

Selling is not a stand-alone function to be performed at either the beginning or the end of a project. For the evangelist to work effectively, it's critical that they know the 'product' intimately. This means a complete understanding of the project and its aims. It's important to involve the evangelist in the project as much as all the other team members. Like everyone else, they need to be true believers, so they're pumped to deliver the right message to the right people at the right time.

Finance

The finance person watches the numbers like a hawk. He/she keeps a close eye on costs, and is always looking for revenue, return on investment, and profit.

Many intrapreneurs find it challenging to work with 'bean counters'. Like it or not, the finance person has a critical role to play in making the project real. These people invariably occupy strategically important positions in the organisation in terms of potential leverage. It's possible, indeed it's imperative, to find a like-minded (okay, similarly-minded) finance person to have on your side.

Just because a person is in a financial role doesn't automatically make them hard to deal with. They're people too, which means they have passions and values just like the rest of us. It's your job to find what floats their boats, and to do whatever it takes to make it happen.

Photo: Sanja Gjenero

Make sure you listen to their advice and concerns. The bottom line is, the world continues to place a lot of emphasis on the bottom line, and there's no sign of that changing any time soon. Having a great finance person on your side to help you present your project in a financially literate and compelling way will go a long way towards ensuring its ultimate success.

Outsider

An outsider provides fresh insights, off-the-cuff observations, and perspectives that aren't available from team members who are, understandably, intimately focused on the project.

Because the outsider has a fresh mindset, and is emotionally detached from the project, he/she can often bring much-needed clarity to the table – perceptions, opinions and suggestions that might take other team members a long time to discover, if ever.

To find your outsider, get out there and talk to people about your project, your passions and your goals! Talk to anyone who'll listen, without fear or embarrassment. Most people are genuinely honourable. You might be pleasantly surprised by what you learn.

Storytelling is a great way to obtain confirmation that your idea has the power to fly, and that you're not obsessing over something that is, at best, only tangential to reality. At the end of the day, rely on your gut instincts when deciding whether it's okay to talk to a stranger. When in doubt, err on the side of choosing not to say as much.

Cultivating a spirit of abundance without compromising confidentiality.

You need a healthy balance between being able to comfortably and passionately discuss your idea with just about anyone, without at the same time giving the whole game away. This is a mixture of faith, live performance, passion and the judicious filtering of information!

> If needs be, create a sanitised, stranger-safe version of your story without killing all the passion and excitement. This is a fun creative exercise in itself!

Muse

This is a very special person, and all intrapreneurs should strive to find at least one in their lives. They can be a life partner or a very close friend, or possibly a long-term coach or mentor.

A muse is someone who's there to listen to you. In this person's presence, you're able to freely bounce, reflect and shape ideas, raise concerns, and troubleshoot challenges. You can do all this without fear of judgement, or making a fool of yourself. A muse is someone you trust implicitly, with whom you can share just about anything. A safe and non-judgemental relationship is critical for moments of creative reflection.

Finding a muse isn't easy. Sometimes they emerge from long-term friendships. Sometimes they simply pop up out of the blue. Suffice it to say, be open to meeting people, and have faith that your muse will arrive when the time is right. Here's to the power of serendipity and joyful coincidences!

> *"I had the great fortune of meeting my muse Helen Richards when I was at university in the early 90s. Her insights, creativity and friendship over the years have contributed immeasurable value to my work and personal growth. Everyone needs their own Helen!"* Zern

Working with realness

Having assembled your dream team, it's time to leverage the team's various strengths while finding ways to compensate for any weaknesses. It's up to you to discover the potential, build the synergy, and lead your team to greatness.

Working with people demands authenticity on your part. You need to be confident you know who you are, and what you're about. This in turn enables you to be open and accepting of others, and to be truly inclusive of differences. Remember, everyone is different, and it is this diversity that powers true innovation.

Establish clear channels of communication, and ensure that these remain open at all times. Bear in mind that different people work better using different methods of communication. Some prefer emails, others the phone, or face-to-face interaction.

Know your team's tolerance and thresholds in terms of crisis management, boredom, and pace of change, and their key drivers/motivators. Again, people have different thresholds in these areas, and respond differently to various types of motivation.

Encourage people to take responsibility for their choices and their actions. Create an environment in which they feel safe to voice their truths and concerns freely. Watch for, and manage, any signs of harassment, bullying or coercion, both within the team and from outside.

Are you a psychopath?

A psychopath is not necessarily violent. Psychopathic behaviour can be said to be an extreme lack of emotional intelligence.

You could be a psychopath if you exhibit these characteristics: you demand that others bend to suit your requirements because you are absolute in your belief that your way is exactly the right way; you're unable to see things from others' points of view; you don't care how your actions affect others; you're aggressive and abusive when dealing with people who disagree with you; you're superficially charming and always say the "right" things, but when things go wrong, it is never your responsibility; you have a different set of rules for yourself and for others.

It's worth learning to be aware of your own actions, and how they could be perceived by others. Sometimes, it's easy to assume that everyone knows without a doubt your good intentions, and is totally in sync with where you want to go. Unfortunately, this isn't always the reality. Just because you have an honourable cause that you're pursuing with a passion doesn't grant you permission to act disrespectfully towards your team. Sometimes, passion can turn into aggressive bullying, when the intrapreneur becomes obsessed with driving his/her cause at the cost of respect and care for the people around them. This is a sure-fire way to lose your team!

You don't have to like everyone you work with, but you can, and should, choose to treat them with respect. Working with realness means tolerance, patience, and often, compromise. Compromise is part of life. The question is – how much to compromise, and when.

> **Compromise can lead to mediocrity! Beware of being drawn into a spiralling series of small, seemingly insignificant compromises that eventually and catastrophically produce a mediocre outcome!**
>
> **When you lose sight of the big picture of what you are trying to achieve, and compromising becomes an end in itself (to keep the project moving), you end up with a decision-by-committee result. Not good. You can say No!**

Sleeping with the enemy

Reality is, you probably don't have a lot of choice over who you get to work with in the wider organisation. Therefore, you need to know how you can get cool stuff done with a whole bunch of different types of people. It helps to understand some of the people-challenges you'll be up against.

Can't-doers

These are people who have developed the ability to construct rock-solid arguments against doing anything into an art-form. "This does not conform to our branding." "The board will never buy this." "That does not integrate with our existing systems." They always look at the negative side of everything, and are driven by fear and resentment.

They may initially seem to be thoughtful and cautious planners. But it soon becomes clear that they have a great aversion to any risk and any change. There's a big difference between the ability to be appropriately cautious, and the inability (or unwillingness) to consider anything!

Sometimes, can't-doers are also motivated by jealousy of you and your ideas. They would rather trash yours than spend the time and energy coming up with their own.

Some can't-doers even try to befriend you in order to prevent you from going through with your ideas. Their mating call is usually "I'm only trying to help", and they just want you to reconsider, before you do anything silly that might jeopardise your career.

Hard as it may seem, try to genuinely listen to everything they say, but don't automatically buy into their arguments. Try to help them see the positives of your project if given the opportunity. Are there real lessons for you in the points they're making?

Develop a healthy 'can't-doer radar', so when you encounter one, you don't let them push your buttons or take up too much of your time. Be aware of their agenda, and resist the temptation to react out of spite or vindictiveness, no matter what they do or say. Just smile, be nice, and walk away.

Long-term-tenured

These are people who've been working for the organisation since the wheel was invented. They're steeped in 'the way things are done around here', having been doing it that way forever. They may have contributed a lot to the organisation over the decades, and have probably built their own little fiefdoms. But they're not even remotely interested in changing things, because according to them, everything's just fine.

Respect them. After all, they've slogged it out, and quite likely did indeed do some fine things in their day. They might prove to be a surprising resource in ways that you can't anticipate. Remember: they know more about how things were done than you! Some of these guys are walking encyclopaedias on the organisation, the industry and the market. Take a softly, softly approach. Make them feel important, empowered, and a valued contributor to the change process. Selectively seek and listen to their input, but don't buy in to their complacency.

Photo: Rachel Fuller

Nowists

These people only see what's in front of them. They don't have the patience, imagination or vision to see the value in, let alone contribute to, something extraordinary over a longer period.

They say things like: "I don't care about the future, what's in it for me now?" They tend to be focused on immediate gains, and are more concerned with actions that have close-quarter influence.

Show them how your project is making a positive contribution in the short term, or at least the short-to-medium term. Show them how your project addresses their immediate concerns. The real challenge is in introducing such a person to the bigger picture.

Invite them to think about the more significant longer-term benefits of your project. If they support you now, what real benefits can they reasonably expect in the next quarter, or next year? That can help focus their mind. Who knows, in the process, you may well introduce a nowist to his/her first glimpse of the world as seen from a height of 10,000 kilometres!

Freeze-and-milkers

These people want to commercialise things way too soon, because they can see a viable business forming (read a truckload of money). They storm onto the scene, and attempt to impose a whole range of management and administrative controls, which invariably results in the fledgling intraprise suffering a near-death experience, or worse.

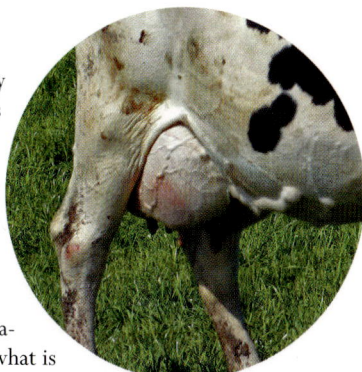
Photo: Alan Belmer

Freeze-and-milkers want to stop (freeze) innovation and change, so as to better exploit (milk) what is there now for as much money as they can get.

Freeze-and-milkers will come armed with a whole sackful of business reasons to justify their actions. You will hear 'responsibility for building shareholder value' repeatedly. What these people invariably fail to recognise is that the controls and limits that they are so desperate to introduce are the very things that, the absence of which, enabled the innovation to occur in the first place! Indeed, they often bear a striking resemblance to the people who dismissed your embryonic idea way back when.

Use a roadmap to show how things could and should progress. Show them you have thought about and planned the process from initial idea through to full commercialisation. Show them what the big-picture payback looks like if your project is allowed to evolve as planned. At this point, all they can see is dollar signs, so make sure that you've got a detailed, logical plan promising impressive and sustainable (and real) long-term benefits to sooth their fevered minds. Remind them that it's critical that innovation be allowed to continue, to avoid stagnation and to stay way ahead of the competition.

Converting enemies to allies

Sometimes, this is possible! Sometimes, a person who is, at first impression, an enemy, turns out to be a staunch ally. You need to be willing to approach even a potential enemy with an open attitude (as you are with any other person), to talk genuinely and passionately about your project.

Did someone mention a mentor?

A mentor is a valuable asset, someone to help you stay focused and on track.

A mentor is usually someone senior within the organisation, someone who has more experience, and most likely a bigger and better-connected network. Your mentor may have been an intrapreneur themselves at some point in his/her career, indeed may still be one, and therefore has a deep understanding of how an intrapreneur thinks and feels, and the challenges they face. Your mentor may even be able to pull a few strings from time to time to assist you.

Photo: Sarah Williams

How do you spot allies? A good place to start is by tracking down fellow colleagues who've made suggestions for improvements. Collect a group of people who can give you a complete range of strengths in terms of the profiles outlined earlier. Don't look for people based solely on rank — you're just as likely to find the people you need in the trenches. And when you find them, nurture and encourage them within an inch of their lives.

Useful resources

American Chamber of Commerce – www.amcham.com.au

Australian Businesswomen's Network – www.abn.org.au

Australian Business Limited – www.australianbusiness.com.au

Australian Institute of Company Directors – www.companydirectors.com.au

Australian Institute of Management – www.aim.com.au

Australian Institute of Office Professionals – www.aiop.com.au

Australian Marketing Institute – www.ami.org.au

Australian Human Resources Institute – www.ahri.com.au

Business Network International – www.bni.com.au

Business Enterprise Centres – www.beca.org.au

Business Referral Group – www.businessreferralgroup.com.au

Cubicle Commando Events – www.cubiclecommando.com.au

Connect Marketing Professionals – www.connectnetwork.com.au

Entrepreneur's Network – www.networxevents.com.au

Females in Information Technology and Telecommunications – www.fitt.org.au

First Wednesday Club – www.abacusrecruit.com.au

Institute of Management Consultants – www.imc.org.au

Last Thursday Club – www.lastthursdayclub.net

Meetings Industry Association of Australia – www.miaanet.com.au

National Speakers Association of Australia – www.nationalspeakers.asn.au

Networking to Win – www.networkingtowin.com.au

Professions Australia – www.professions.com.au

Recruitment Consulting Services Association – www.rcsa.com.au

Rural Women's Network – www.agric.nsw.gov.au

Social Enterprise Network – www.social-e.org.au

Sydney Talks – www.sydneytalks.com.au

The CEO Institute – www.ceo.com.au

The Innovation Council – www.innovation.gov.au

Thought Leaders – www.thoughtleaders.com.au

Volunteering Australia – www.volunteeringaustralia.org

Women Chiefs of Enterprise – www.wcei.com.au

Women in Finance – www.wifnsw.com.au

Women's Network Australia – www.womensnetwork.com.au

Youth 2 Youth – www.youth2youth.com.au

Joie de Vivre Hospitality

Chip Conley, CEO

Joie de Vivre is the second largest boutique hotelier in the world with 35 boutique hotels created over the past twenty years. With nearly 2,500 employees and more than 4,000 guest rooms, Joie de Vivre serves more than a million hotel guests per year providing an approach to service that has won the company numerous awards from the "Experience Stager of the Year" (an award which JDV won over Disney and Cirque du Soleil) to "E-Marketer of the Year" worldwide to "Guerrilla Marketer of the Year."

Joie de Vivre has set itself apart within the hospitality industry by taking a conceptual approach to the creation of its hotels and restaurants. From the cinema-inspired Hotel Bijou, to the arts and literary infused Hotel Rex, to the Hotel Del Sol, a lively "boutique motel", each property possesses its own dynamic personality. We focus on the 'psychographics', versus the 'demographics ' of our guests.

Joie de Vivre's unique approach to creating its boutique hotels is based upon the idea that each hotel is created in the image of a niche-oriented magazine. Starting with the Phoenix, which is based upon Rolling Stone magazine, Joie de Vivre uses 5 words that describe the magazine to influence the creation of the hotel concept.

Phoenix's décor, services and amenities, and overall identity is influenced by the 5 words that describe Rolling Stone.

What we've learned over time is that our boutique hotels are mirrors for their most loyal customers. The words these customers would use to describe their favorite hotel are the same words they'd use to describe themselves. This is why we introduced Yvette, the Hotel Matchmaker on the home page of our website as a means of helping guests find the perfect hotel to fit their personality.

One of the things that makes me most proud of Joie de Vivre is that during good times or bad, we stick to our basic business model which is depicted by the heart icon since our whole team provides service from the heart. This business model is based upon the premise that creating a unique corporate culture makes you money. Happy employees translate to happy customers. The staff-authored mission statement, "Creating opportunities to celebrate the joy of life," says it all. The company also gives away more than 1,200 room nights per year to community groups and raises $1 million annually for philanthropic activities primarily related to the issues of youth-at-risk, AIDS and cancer health organizations, homelessness, and arts & culture.

www.jdvhospitality.com

CEO Chip's Conley's first book, THE REBEL RULES, came out in 2001 and had a Foreword written by Virgin's Richard Branson. He has a book coming out in October 2006 called MARKETING THAT MATTERS: 10 PRACTICES TO PROFIT YOUR BUSINESS AND CHANGE THE WORLD and another one coming out in September 2007 called PEAK: HOW GREAT COMPANIES GET THEIR "MOJO" FROM MASLOW.

Here're some of the things we do to foster intrapreneurs:

(1) Take a retreat, but not just with your managers... take the whole staff and let the line level team feel that their fingerprints are all over the company's strategy.

(2) Reward people for great ideas... a few years back, we had an idea of the month award company-wide.

(3) Follow the golden rule... we create "Dreammakers" for our guests which are thoughtful little customized experiences or gifts upon arrival that are perfectly suited to that particular guest...so for the JDV employee who does the best Dreammaker of the month, we reciprocate and come up with a customized gift for that employee that's perfectly suited for them.

(4) Boss for a day... some of our hotel General Managers have chosen to anoint one of their biggest troublemakers (i.e., rebels) as the boss for the day to run the hotel operations – it's a good way to harness all that troublemaker energy and it usually leads to the person having a newfound respect for their boss, the General Manager.

(5) CEO Quarterly Supper... I have a big dinner once per quarter that any employee in the company can come to...it's an informal affair which allows employees to come and share ideas.

(6) "How to Start Your Own Business" class... I've taught this class every 2-3 years (doing so again this summer) – most companies would be frightened to teach this class as they'd feel they would be encouraging their employees to leave, but the better question to ask is "What is encouraging entrepreneurs to join our company?"....the issue isn't people leaving, it's attracting people who might not ever join you if you have too traditional a work environment...we like to think of our company as an "incubator for entrepreneurs"...many folks have come here for 3-7 years, learned everything they can and gone out to create their own business – we have yet to incubate an entrepreneur who after leaving us did something that was competitively problematic for us.

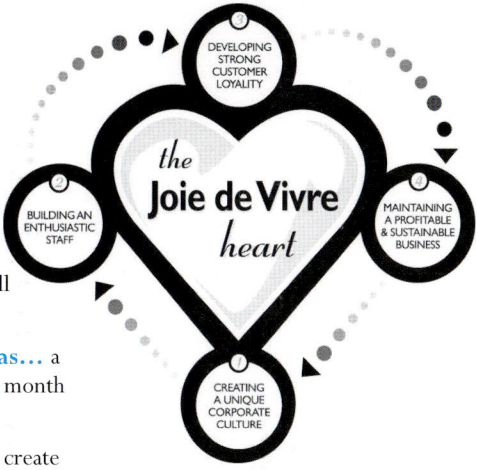

the **Joie de Vivre** *heart*

DEVELOPING STRONG CUSTOMER LOYALITY

BUILDING AN ENTHUSIASTIC STAFF

MAINTAINING A PROFITABLE & SUSTAINABLE BUSINESS

CREATING A UNIQUE CORPORATE CULTURE

Photo: Tanja Sund

4. Teams

The conventional concept of a team player can be limited
– and limiting. Artificially enthused team-building is often
a waste of time. There's too much focus on superficial
conformity, which breeds non-challenging, consensus-
driven workplaces and work practices, where platitudes
and weasel words abound.

Teamwork is about working constructively with a whole
range of individuals with unique needs, personal goals,
emotions, fears, triggers, and values. You need to relate to
people in business as you do in life. Treat them with
respect. Listen to them. Be prepared to give and take.
Make them feel valued.

"Leaders don't force people to follow. They invite them on a journey."

Charles Lauer

People's attitude is way more important than their skills. It makes ALL the difference. What's important is that you get big-picture buy-in from them. Understand that not everyone is a traditional team player – which is actually a great opportunity. It's no use having a flock of sycophantic 'yes persons' on your team.

How do you acknowledge, celebrate and leverage the differences in opinions and approaches among team members? Is this even welcomed in your projects?

Creating buy-in

We're talking about total buy-in here – heart, mind, body and soul – the full monty. Not only from your dream team, but also from the wider organisation and other people you meet along the way!

The best way to get people firing on all cylinders is to present a vision and a cause that inspires and excites them. To keep them pumping, it's important to ensure that everyone's voice is heard, respected, and acknowledged. Everyone needs to feel valued.

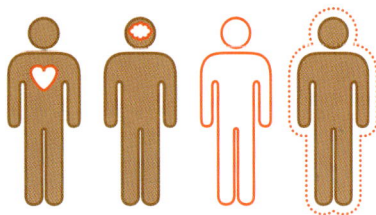

Photo: Levi Szekeres

Unfortunately, most organisations continue to employ the traditional command and control model, which just doesn't cut it. They forget, or don't understand, that buy-in is an emotion thing. You cannot create loyalty and commitment with a contract.

The first step towards obtaining buy-in involves capturing the mind. Most people are programmed to apply logic when assessing new ideas, so it's important to outline what you're trying to do in logical, easily-understood terms. You also need to be a role model, leading the way, observing the behaviour of those around you, and providing positive feedback.

Don't forget the heart though, because real buy-in will only occur when both hearts and minds are engaged. More often than not, we're trained to work solely with our minds – in particular, with logical, sequential left-brain-directed thinking.

Have you ever been in a situation where everything appears to make logical sense, but you still feel that something's not quite right? That's a sure sign of incomplete buy-in.

Body and soul engagement completes the buy-in picture. This is where full emotional engagement happens. This is when the people you are talking to

> *"One of my best moments was when I was presenting my version of a client's vision back to them for confirmation; and one of them said 'Stop! You're going to make me cry!'"* Zern

jump up with excitement. This is when they (and you) get goosebumps and even teary-eyed because of your moving vision and cause. The secret to this is – you need to feel it too!

Engaging through vision

A vision is a great starting point. Visions inspire hope. Hope makes people feel that they have a sense of purpose from which they can derive meaning. A vision is the ultimate description of the manifestation of an idea.

Paradoxically, visions are like mirages. They draw you forward, but as you draw close to each one, they are likely to disappear, only to be replaced by another, even more exciting one further away! There's never going to be a finishing line, and that's the great thing about visions. The journey is the whole point.

Photo: Zern Liew

You can never please everyone of course. The moment you decide to try to please everyone is the moment you become bland and mediocre, or book yourself a one-way ticket to the funny-farm.

Visions shouldn't just be feel-good statements loaded with trendy tokenism. Visions (and values) have to be felt and loved, and not simply given lip-service. Some examples of organisations whose visions you can really feel are: Virgin, Louis Vuitton, Nudie, The Body Shop, Absolut, and Google.

Visions can attract like a magnet, or repel like fly spray. It's about working with love marks – getting the total emotional connection. People will either love you or hate you, depending on how they perceive your vision.

When your team members feel inspired by your vision, and feel involved, respected and valued, it's highly likely that your team will develop close ties, providing an example that can flow through to the rest of the organisation, and even beyond.

Vision statements are just feel-good, woo-woo, new-age things. Who really gets them, anyway? And they're so vague and long-term. Tell them they're dreaming. Let's focus on the here and now – on what's real. Our vision is some crappy framed piece of paper hanging on the wall that doesn't mean squat. I don't feel it. Every year the bosses unveil a new vision, but it's all just so much run-of-the-mill weasel-pee. Problem is, I have no choice but to toe the line, right?

A vision guides everything. It unites people, and elevates them to a higher emotional level. This usually translates into extraordinary outcomes. People feel part of the organisation, part of a community that's united in working for the common good.

Of course you have a choice. Choose to create a truly moving version of the vision for yourself.

Photos: Rachel Fuller

Exercise: Are you living your own vision or someone else's?

An intrapreneur's project is an intraprise, a mini-business. With that in mind, you need to sit down and work out your vision before you start. Think about the moment when you finally achieve your goals; what does the vision of that look, smell and feel like? It's well worth your while taking the time to write a detailed and emotionally engaging description of your vision. Review it, sleep on it, think about it, talk about it, then edit and rewrite it. If you're a visual thinker, draw diagrams, or create a collage of images representing the emotions behind your vision.

It's important to link your project's vision to the organisation's mission and goals, and to align it with the organisation's values. This increases both the likelihood of broad-scale buy-in, and the possibility of different teams coming together on various projects as new opportunities emerge.

Authentic values

These are your morals – your guiding principles in life. They should be evident in absolutely everything you do: from strategies, processes, actions, communication and marketing, through to document design and how you answer the phone. They must be clearly evident in every aspect of your project!

> Think of your organisation as a person. What are its values? What are yours? Do they align? Your values are your personal moral compass. Comparing your values to those of your organisation can be a great way to see if you are suited to each other.

Values aren't just feel-good words hanging on the wall. They cannot be created by a committee, but rather must come from within the project driver – i.e. you! Being clear about, and staying true to, your values is what makes all the difference when working with people.

Whether we're conscious of it or not, we react positively to authenticity. It's odd how the conventional business world eschews authenticity for the 'toeing the corporate line' mentality. And then spends millions on we-care feel-good advertising in a desperate attempt to fix the lack-of-authenticity problem.

A cause

A cause is the reason you get out of bed on Mondays. The reason why your project is worthwhile. It's the ultimate, emotionally charged, value proposition of your intraprise.

You need to be working towards your cause every day. It's the driver of the intraprise. It decides whether you take on certain clients, projects, or research. It's what can put you into a new market – one that you can create and dominate, rather than being a me-too player. It's about surpetition – rising above merely competing with others to be in your own race.

Having a cause is a great way to describe the fundamental value-add of your project. If you did not proceed with this project, what would your organisation or its clients miss out on? How will your project make the world a better place, even if it only affects one person in one department on the other side of the world?

Apart from being a great way to connect with people, your cause is also your decision-making yardstick. Every decision you make should be measured against your cause to see if it is truly in alignment. If something doesn't support your cause, don't do it! If someone hasn't bought in to your cause, keep them at a distance!

Example: Think of your project as a verb. To do this effectively, you first need a funky project name. For example: Swish. When you're trying to make a decision, ask yourself: Is this a Swish thing to do? When thinking about the impact your project is making, ask yourself: Have I 'swished' this issue?

Common enemy

Brave projects invariably attract enemies. Enemies are great to have. They offer a fine way to create buy-in. "We need to be better than them." "Let's show them we can do it!" "United we stand…".

We're not talking about enemies in the context of an imminent threat. You don't have to go out and poison their water cooler, or barricade yourselves in a corner of the office! Indeed, some of your team members may well work for the enemy! Which is okay. The concept of an enemy we are talking about here is simply another useful tool you can use to cultivate buy-in, and maintain team focus.

Your enemy could be another project team with conflicting values and goals. It could be an edict delivered from senior management that threatens your project. It could be something a competitor is doing or planning to do, or it could be a wider social issue.

It's worth spending some time with your team establishing a common enemy. Find one that invigorates your team, and inspires them to go the extra distance. Herein lies the key to using an enemy as a buy-in tool: it's all about inspiration, not competition.

Photo: Levi Szekeres

Beware the trap of competing with, and reacting to, your common enemy. Ultimately, this can cause you to become a reactive follower, rather than a trailblazing revolutionary.

Impossible missions

BHAGs are another great way to create buy-in to your project. "They say – you can't do that." We say – "Just watch us!"

BHAGs inspire people to go way beyond the call of duty to produce results that they never thought they could. The combined efforts of inspired, talented and focused individuals, powered by a shared BHAG, can be mind-blowing. Imagine how the folks at NASA felt back in the early 60s when President Kennedy announced that they were going to put a man on the moon by the end of the decade. Say what? But they did it. And so began a journey that to date has resulted in

Big, Hairy, Audacious Goals

around 1400 inventions that have improved the quality of life for those of us back on Earth, including kidney dialysis machines, CAT scanning technology, freeze-dried food, sound insulation for vehicles, water purification technology, metal surface coatings, food packaging, protective suits worn by race-car drivers and hazardous area workers, reflective blankets, cordless power tools and appliances, and hazardous gas sensors.

Openness and acceptance

If you believe the statements on the right, and you should, you need to start cultivating a mindset of openness and acceptance to life, in order to start gathering these gifts from people around you.

Everyone has something to offer. There's value in every idea.

Being open and accepting is a very powerful way to obtain buy-in for your project, your ideas, and yourself as an individual. This inclusive attitude allows you to appeal to the fundamental need of everyone to be heard and acknowledged,

An open and accepting team environment is critical to facilitating togetherness. It means listening to, and valuing, all input from everyone. The more ideas that are on the table, the better. This whole thing is about ideas, after all!

Being open to every idea does not of course mean every idea must be implemented exactly as it was first articulated. Ideas are infinitely malleable; they undergo transformation, and lead to other possibilities. If not here and now, where, when, and how else? Trying to incorporate everyone's ideas is like trying to design a horse using a committee. Hey, cute camel!

Photo: Yvan Lagarrigue

Cultivating the intention and attitude within yourself to be open requires real self-confidence. Get over the need to prove yourself. Or to be right. You're okay as you are. You don't need to have the final say!

Suspense and mystery

When communicating your project to the wider organisation (or the world), think about spinning some intrigue and mystery around your story.

Keeping people informed as to your progress is important of course. People outside your project team need to know that something interesting is happening. But you should also maintain a certain degree of secrecy, just to keep the curiosity levels up.

A funky project name can be the easiest thing to create some suspense and mystery around your project.

What do you think the following projects are about? Are you curious?

Cattleprod. Jonathan, Killandra, Vivavo, Hop, Collup.

Most people love a surprise, so long as it's pleasant. By holding something back, you can give them this when the project outcomes are finally revealed.

Some ideas for creating mystery are: refer to your project by a funky name; create your own secret code words and acronyms; spin some hype about celebrity endorsement; subtly talk about aspects of the project wherever you go to prod and enthuse. Create a cult-like suspense. This is great fun and as outsiders become excited, you'll find it will inspire and excite you even more!

Beware of creating too much secrecy and aloofness though. The key here is not to come across as an elite group that's been hand-picked to work on a super-special project.

Having a team secret helps everyone pull together! Remember the last time you were involved in planning a surprise party?

Photo: Melissa Balkon

Reward your team

Look at what's important to each team member. What motivates them? Way too many companies focus solely on financial rewards, or offer standard incentives that don't do it for many people for any number of reasons. For example one company we know rewards all staff with bottles of Moet — what about those who don't drink? Think of all those silly meaningless awards that are given out to employees every quarter...

People need rewards and encouragement. They need to know that they're on the right track, and that their contribution is valued. If you care, they will too, but you need to show them. They're not mind-readers. No combination of money and perks can match the deep and enduring satisfaction of knowing that one's talent is making a difference, and is truly appreciated.

When it comes to heart-felt rewards, it's always the thought and genuine intent that counts. Never do it for the sake of doing it!

Rewards can include:

Recognition for achievement	Status and prestige
Freedom to express innate creativity	Power and authority to make decisions
Ethical satisfaction	Sense of organisational achievement
Being part of a team	Pleasant work environment
Intellectual stimulation	Flexible work conditions
Variety	Family-friendly workplaces
Financial compensation	Learning opportunities

Photo: Konstantinos Dafalias

Staying in alignment

It's difficult not to over-emphasise the importance of staying true to your cause and vision. You need to constantly check back on, reinforce, and reiterate your cause and vision throughout the course of the project.

Even if you're not on the Board, and therefore unable to directly influence the wider organisation's vision, values and cause, you still need to establish these for your intraprise. Incidentally, if you haven't already done so, we strongly suggest you create a vision and cause for your own life!

Most project management techniques focus on deadlines, deliverables and out-comes. You can prepare specification documents, budgets, and Gantt and Pert charts until the cows come home, but if you ignore people's emotions, you'll struggle to achieve alignment, engagement, and ongoing buy-in.

Use your cause, your values and your vision to obtain buy-in and maintain momentum. And check in with your team regularly. In your get-togethers, which don't have to be formal or regular but should be frequent, tell more stories. Review what your enemies are doing, and what you're doing about that. Celebrate your successes and failures together.

Maintaining momentum

Without momentum, the team will fall apart. So, how can you keep things humming along? How about taking the team out for lunch, giving them all $200 to spend, and then sending them off for an hour, after which everyone gathers to celebrate their purchases – this takes people back to the childhood joy of show-and-tell. A round of golf or paintball can also do the trick. Whatever you do, it's important to include all members of the team, and ensure that everyone bonds together well. It's also important not to play favourites. Open minds, mutual respect and freedom of expression can produce amazing synergies.

Don't forget – being accepting also means you need to respect that some members of your team may hate team-building days. Do make allowances for that. Beware of letting team-building exercises become ends in themselves (as they often do). What you do is not important. It's how everyone feels about doing something together, and about each other as people afterwards that is the point.

Keep deadlines happening

Deadlines are more than just a date on a document or wall-chart. Ambitious deadlines can be used as an effective tool to keep momentum going. Looming deadlines keep the focus strong, and can serve to bond people together. Send out for some pizza and drinks, crank up the music, and watch your team get wildly energetic and creative.

Don't get too ambitious though, driving your team so hard that everyone collapses from exhaustion. Develop empathy, and learn to read the mood of the meeting. Like so many things in life, balance is the key.

You can lose yourself in the details of your project. It is not a good thing to get so obsessed with your project that the rest of your life starts to unravel, or you start treating people and yourself badly for the sake of the project. Are you unhappy and stressed most of the time? Do you often find yourself pushing and driving your team hard to meet deadlines as opposed to calmly and productively working towards exciting goals? Maybe it is time to stop and ease off a bit. What can you shift off your plate right now?

Photo: T Taudigani

Know when to allow time to reflect, and when it's time to fire up with action. Be realistic in your expectations – nothing's ever perfect. When it's good enough to ship, seize the moment and ship!

Sometimes it is more important to keep the action flowing than stop for details. Beware the paralysis-by-analysis or death-by-perfection syndromes. Excessive focus on total perfection can delay projects and cause momentum to slip. The detail may be important, but don't forget the big picture.

Regular updates

Create a passionate culture where there's anticipation and excitement in the air by providing regular updates on progress.

Photo: Nick Lobeck

Regular meetings help. Too boring? Give them a makeover. Don't just stand and deliver from a standard reporting template. Make them interactive and productive. Encourage input from everyone. Again, freedom to speak without fear, and respect for all, is what matters. This will help you to keep abreast of team priorities and key drivers, and is a constant potential source of ideas for further innovation.

Cool newsletters are also a great way to stay connected. Again, don't fall into the familiar pattern of forcing someone who doesn't want to write it to chase contributions from people who don't care. If you've only got one thing to say, leave it at that. And then ask a question, or throw in a brainteaser. Want interaction? Set up a blog.

Celebrate and commiserate

Celebration of significant successes AND failures is a critical part of the innovation process. They're important landmarks, and present learning opportunities to build upon for future adventures.

Celebrating successes is pretty easy, but make sure that you also have some sort of positive ritual for dealing with failures. No blame-games, no finger pointing, no tantrums. Your team will not only appreciate your dedication to pursuing extraordinary results, but everyone will learn extremely valuable lessons while continuing to feel good about themselves, even when things aren't totally hunky dory.

When we say failure, we are talking about failures resulting from uncontrollable and un-anticipatable situations. Instances where, despite your best efforts, something untoward still happened. There is another kind of failure, one that happens due to carelessness or negligence. When faced with one of these, do take steps to address those problems directly and constructively with the people involved. Everyone makes mistakes, but the only way we learn is if someone points them out to us!

As part of your project communications plan, present a list of what worked and what didn't, and why, every month or quarter.

Back to basics

Tell the stories again – re-discover the original passion. Invite input – no recriminations, no grudges. Has something changed? Did you miss something? Invite others to tell their own stories. Use pictures, music and dance.

Take time out, step back and review the project from afar. Is it still valid? Maybe it's time to abandon it. Even if this is the case, search for the learning. Remember Edison?

The importance of story telling:

We all love stories – from Mum or Dad tucking us up in bed at night when we were children, to the latest Hollywood big-screen surround-sound blockbuster. Stories work because they engage our minds and our hearts. Stories are an easy way to pass on complex information – we humans have been doing it for thousands of years!

Photo: Griszka Niewiadomski

The elements of a good story:

An intriguing beginning, empathy (with the key character), challenge and conflict (with a good dose of emotions), and (a triumphant or tragic) conclusion.

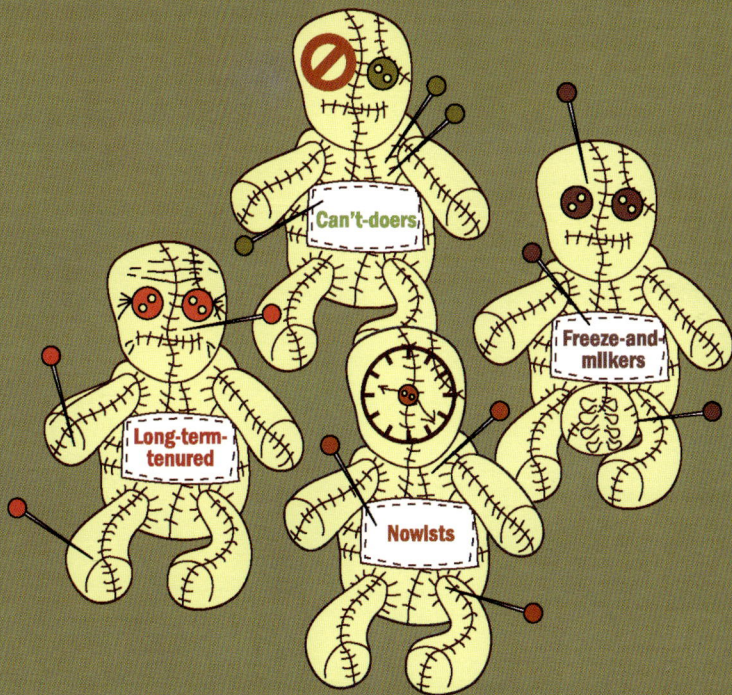

Can't-doers

Long-term-tenured

Freeze-and-milkers

Nowists

Enemies can hurt your team-building efforts. Read Chapter 3 to learn about these enemies and how to deal with them.

Australland

Chris Warrell, General Manager, Human Resources

I learnt the hard way that while you need to be able to talk the language of the corporation, your core values and beliefs can't be compromised.

Businesses need to focus on inputs, not outputs. There's too much focus on profitability, and not enough on creativity. People need clarity of purpose, a sense of connection, and a clear structure of responsibility and support to work in – profits will then flow.

When people work through definitive challenges, they emerge more self-assured and more aware of others, and this can often provide the catalyst for change.

When I joined Australland, the focus was on building apartments, and building profit. Now we're busy building the human component into the organisation, because employees need to feel a sense of giving something back, to feel engaged, that there is a greater purpose, and that they're not just working for the sake of it.

We've introduced clarity, awareness and paybacks by implementing initiatives such as a counselling service for staff, their partners and their kids that the company pays for, and it's making the world of difference to employees' lives. It's necessary to provide these things in order to be competitive in attracting the best people. We want to create an environment that positions Australland as the employer of choice for all aspiring property professionals.

People with questioning attributes, intrapreneurs, generally have a huge amount of energy. This can be confronting to their less energetic colleagues, but it's an important resource, and these people should be used as internal change agents. Organisations need to accept the inevitability of, and be prepared for, challenge and change. The reality is that many companies struggle with innovation, when they should be encouraging and embracing it.

The biggest challenge is that people think 'support and encourage' is soft. There needs to be an attitudinal shift, because you can't get the best out of people by controlling them – you need to engage them.

There's going to be serious competition for talent, so employers need to embrace intrapreneurs and the creativity and innovation they offer in order to compete. Many Gen Yers are intrapreneurs, with different attitudes that need to be accommodated and celebrated!

You can encourage people to think differently, but you can't force them to innovate. What you can do is weave intrapreneurs into the fabric of the organisation. Everybody has the ability to think differently if placed in the right environment. It's all about the culture of the place – how managers recognise that it is a constant journey, and that they need to assist people by empowering them with self-confidence.

You must believe passionately in what you're doing, and in what you know, but understand that change needs to happen incrementally. It can't happen in one big bang, or the corporation will implode and lose people – you need to bring people on the journey.

Australland is one of Australia's major diversified property groups, with activities across Australia covering development of residential land, housing and apartments, development of and investment in income producing commercial and industrial properties, and property management.

www.australand.com.au

Inverted traditional organisation chart reflects the attitude change from "command & control" to "support of & responsibility to" those above.

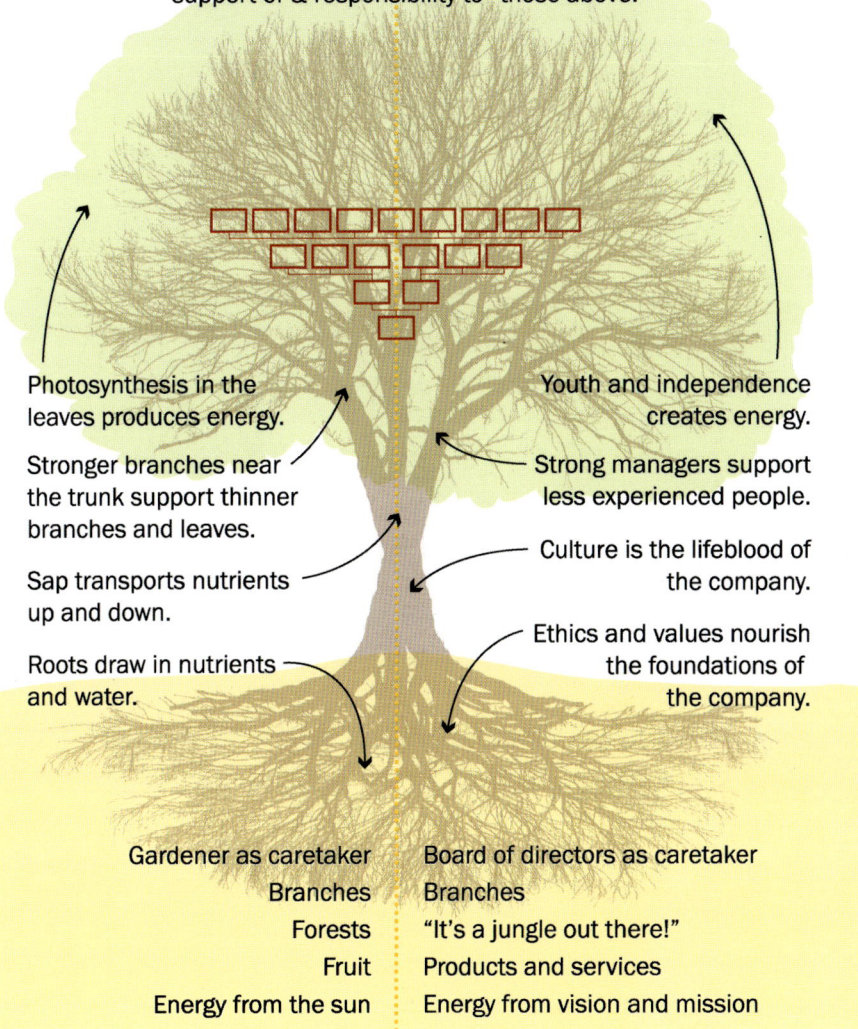

Photosynthesis in the leaves produces energy.

Stronger branches near the trunk support thinner branches and leaves.

Sap transports nutrients up and down.

Roots draw in nutrients and water.

Youth and independence creates energy.

Strong managers support less experienced people.

Culture is the lifeblood of the company.

Ethics and values nourish the foundations of the company.

A Tree	A Company
Gardener as caretaker	Board of directors as caretaker
Branches	Branches
Forests	"It's a jungle out there!"
Fruit	Products and services
Energy from the sun	Energy from vision and mission

Photo: Zern Liew

5. Ideas

It all starts with ideas

Ideas, and the people who generate them, are at the hub of all extraordinary organisations. Without ideas, there would be no new inventions, new products, or new services. Without ideas, everything would stagnate. We'd still be living in caves, wondering how we were going to catch something to eat before it got dark.

Ideas are the major differentiator between competing organisations – the only true source of sustainable competitive advantage. Particularly in today's world, where yesterday's big new thing is so – well, *yesterday*. A world where commoditisation is threatening the economic model in developed societies like never before.

In his book Re-Imagine!, Tom Peters talked about rapid commoditisation and how it is threatening white-collar jobs. Ideas and innovation are the key things we desperately need to go forward; not just competing at the product features level.

Technology is eliminating many jobs forever, and more and more of what remains is being outsourced to cheaper producers. We're moving into a new age, one that demands conceptual thinking and innovation – which all starts with ideas.

In a world that is increasingly end-goal-focused, we let other issues get in the way of the generation of ideas far too often! In our haste to make quick money, and to minimise change (so we can continue to make money without leaving our comfort zone), we fail to allow sufficient time and space to generate the big ideas that can lead to new market opportunities and sustainable long-term profitability.

Don't kill the goose

If an enterprise is successful, all too often greed and fear quickly arrive to take a seat on the Board. The powers-that-be see the business as a once-in-a-lifetime opportunity to make as much money as possible as quickly as possible. They focus on maintaining the status quo, attempting to freeze the business in time. They know it works, although they may not know exactly why, but heck it's making them a pile of money, so don't frighten the horses! Such an attitude can only go so far – it's effectively the beginning of the end. The idea-generation process stagnates. Innovation dies. And as surely as night follows day, somewhere down the track, the organisation, too, draws its final breath.

Someone once said that 'frames trump facts'. Not so long ago, we had two 'facts' – the military had the internet for communicating intelligence (don't get us started on the oxymoron thing!) and there were 'super-computers' (that look like an abacus compared to what we're using today, but that's another story), with the wonderfully prescient (not!) prediction that there was no future for personal computers. Then someone re-framed the situation – and we got the web. How powerful was that idea?

Think about what doctors are now doing – or not doing. They don't do simple things like take a blood sample any more. Someone else does that, and then sends it off to be analysed by a machine. And then, the results are increasingly being sent offshore for interpretation!

Sure, we all have to make money to live. But if we don't value ideas, commoditisation will kill us in the end. And if you think commoditisation only hurts businesses, think again. What does your job entail? Is it easily replicated and transferable? How about to someone as qualified as you, but working in another country for one-tenth of your salary, and over-the-moon at their good fortune? This is exactly what many white-collar professionals are facing right now, and the trend is spreading like wildfire to encompass all kinds of jobs and industries.

Conventional business systems are becoming highly standardised, thanks to 'best-practice' and quality assurance certification processes such as the ISO9000 series of standards. Standardisation means it is becoming increasingly easy to replicate an entire business, at least from a process viewpoint. Witness the boom in franchising over recent times. Franchising is all about systemising and standardising. Many emerging countries do this very well, and at a fraction of the cost. Being able to manufacture something no longer provides significant competitive advantage, at least not in what we patronisingly continue to call the developed world. Someone else can invariably do it cheaper.

Interestingly, the ability to replicate entire businesses elsewhere has led to new ideas in an attempt to prevent unauthorised copying of products. Manufacturing companies are sourcing various components from Asian suppliers, but using a process whereby different parts are made in various countries and then assembled elsewhere, making it harder to copy the finished product. Indeed the manufacturers of the different parts often don't know what the finished product is!

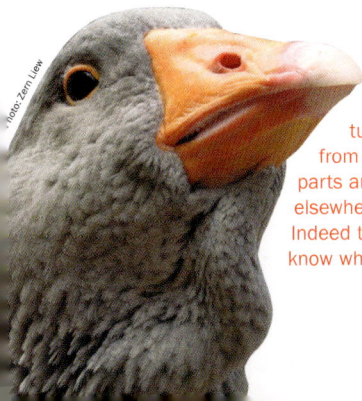

Beware the Best Practice Trap

This concept dovetails very neatly with the culture of non-thinking and fear that permeates many organisations. Their preference is to use what everyone else is already using, on the assumption that it must be good – or at least no worse than what others are using. Thus there is no need to think, or question things. They feel safe, because they have what everyone else has.

Best practice has its place – especially for repeated processes where consistency is important or critical to our lives and wellbeing. But best practice when applied to organisational strategy is certain death in the long run.

All current world records in all sports are 'best practice' and 'industry standard', but that doesn't stop people the world over dedicating their lives to bettering them. Organisations need to adopt the same attitude. Why should the business world be any different!

The only course of action that will prove to be productive and sustainable in the longer term is for organisations to embrace the search for ideas, and to pursue innovation with a passion. The same goes for you as an individual – the most important investment you can make in your career, and in your life, is to nurture and celebrate your creative spirit.

We need to think long-term, three steps ahead of the game. We need people with vision, and the courage to act. We need people who can think beyond the bottom line. The world desperately needs ideas and innovation from intrapreneurs like you to reinvent the game of business. In turn, this will re-shape the world in which we live, and how we interact as a global community.

Ideas are useless unless they have an obvious monetary value. It's all well and good for some of us to sit around navel-gazing trying to come up with cool ideas, but money is the only thing that matters at the end of the day. Leave creativity to the experts, or do it on the weekends if you must!

Everyone's capable of creativity – there are no card-carrying 'experts'. We need to encourage creativity and innovative thinking at all levels of the organisation, because if we don't, we're dead. We need to provide a suitable environment and incentives for innovative thinking. Ideas and imagination are the things that bring fun, passion, learning and communication back into the workplace, and provide the launching pad for an exciting future.

Photos: Rachel Fuller

Ideas are for sharing

From a copyright point of view, ideas that aren't expressed have no actual value. It's only when they're manifested as something tangible, as designs, documents, plans, and actions, that they become valuable.

Ideas are everywhere, and in unlimited abundance. You have a duty to identify them, and then share them!

Be generous with your ideas. Don't hoard them. Throw them out there, because this encourages engagement, feedback, and valueadding from the people you confide in. Ideas are for playing with, for growing and moulding. If someone, anyone, can make an idea come to life, that's better than keeping it secret, and never letting it see the light of day. Without leaving yourself open to exploitation, of course.

Photo: Gaston Thauvin

It's no accident that so much great music was written by collaborators. (And it's no accident that this great book was written by collaborators!)

What collaborative projects, for work or personal enjoyment, are you engaged in right now? Suggestions: write a book with someone, create art together, write an opera,.. Two heads are always better than one, and its great fun sharing ideas and passion!

"Who we become together, will always be different than who we are alone. New relationships create new capacities."

Margaret Wheatley

Umbrellas in summer

Many organisations tend to follow a boom-bust cycle in their search for ideas and innovation. When times are good and the cash is flowing, they find it relatively easy to allocate some resources to ideas and R&D. Then, when the gravy-train starts to run out of steam, they re-think their priorities, and guess where the cuts are made? There's no time to assess the relative merits of various endeavours, and so strong projects showing promising potential, and often within sight of bearing fruit, are abandoned along with the weaker ones (which may yet have proved to be the diamonds in the dirt). So when the competition gets tough, instead of being able to introduce a game-breaking innovation, organisations are caught flat-footed.

It's clear that sustainable innovation requires a new approach. Collaborative entrepreneurship, whereby organisations gain access to the insights and capabilities of other entities, offers exciting possibilities.

Innovation initiatives need to become part of the ongoing commercial dialogue that takes place among organisations. But how can organisations make such sensitive information freely available without giving their competitors an advantage, or at the very least, giving up their own potential competitive advantage? One answer lies in a practice that's been common since the middle ages: the use of intermediaries to broker the exchange of sensitive information among organisations without revealing the identities or motives of their clients, and without otherwise compromising their interests. Such collaboration provides unique opportunities to develop ideas and innovations with the leverage of insights and technologies provided by several organisations.

Don't have access to an intermediary? Be one yourself! Cultivate contacts in other organisations you can trust and open up more with. Share your passion, and tap into theirs.

Whose idea is it anyway?

It can be tempting to think of an idea as mine, or yours; to be jealously guarded, or summarily dismissed respectively. In reality, ideas come from the soup of our past experiences, seasoned by the stimuli around us, and stirred through with our values and beliefs.

Lighten up! Ideas are not something to accrue. There's no ideas bank where you can continually deposit ideas into your personal account. Ideas are meant to be discussed, kneaded and teased. Embrace and engage with ideas for the fun of it. The greatest thing about working with ideas is the pleasure of discussing them with other people!

If you think someone has stolen your idea, don't worry, this happens all the time given the nature of ideas and human interaction (okay, people talk). At least you've received confir-

You can't steal an idea, but you can steal the manifestation of an idea. Plagiarism is stealing. Making or buying bootleg DVDs is stealing.

mation that your idea was great. And it's out there, hopefully on its way to making an impact on the world! Let them run with it. Chances are that they'll take it somewhere you hadn't thought of, and that's a great thing. Look at the lessons they're learning. Can you build on what they're doing? And take your initial idea further, to somewhere even better? Aim to out-innovate them! And was that the only idea you've ever had? Of course not. So keep 'em coming!

Generating ideas

Everyone has the potential to be creative. It's part of what has made our species so successful. Have you ever met a young child who is not creative? And more than happy to prove it at every possible opportunity!

For creativity to flourish, we need permission and time to think. We need the freedom to be able to play. We need to value thinking, rather than attendance and 'busyness'. Is the word business a derivative of busy-ness? Is it any surprise we meet so many adults who think they're probably not very creative, but in any case they haven't got time to find out because they're too busy being busy?

Generating ideas is about playing. Anything goes, as long as the ideas keep coming. Set aside judgement. Encourage your colleagues and team members to speak their minds without fear of censorship or admonishment, and see what emerges. Connect ideas at random. No rules, no logic. Evaluation is a separate exercise that can be done later.

Give yourself permission to stop and think. Set aside some time each day to come up with new ideas. Don't judge these ideas at all. Just have fun playing with them.

Everywhere you look, there are answers. You just have to be asking the right questions.

Be open to all possibilities – there are opportunities everywhere. Why not take a short break right now. Go for a walk, and give yourself permission to think – the wilder and juicier the better. And don't forget to take that notebook and pen, or digital recorder!

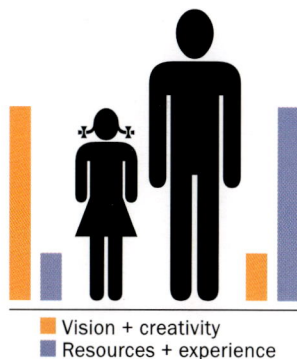

■ Vision + creativity
■ Resources + experience

Everyone is born creative. The problem is, as we 'grow up', we are trained to self-censor our creative, playful thoughts because of fear. Fear of ridicule and alienation. Do you self-censor your thoughts?

Ground rules

The last thing you need during an idea-generation exercise is for people to feel inhibited – unwilling to speak up for fear of judgement, ridicule or censure. This applies equally to your personal brainstorming sessions. Check your ego at the door please!

Make sure everyone feels genuinely heard and valued. And just saying this upfront isn't enough. Your actions have to reflect your stated position. This means engaging actively and equally with everyone in the group. If you're working alone, remember to be kind to yourself, and actively engage with all the different voices in your head, without prejudice or judgement.

Create a safe environment. You're here to generate new ideas, and to have fun in the process. This isn't the place to work through any lingering enmity or resentment. Nor is it the place to engage in factional fights with a view to point-scoring. If you're working alone, make sure you're in a good emotional place to focus on some heavy-duty play!

Identify and manage any bullies in the group. These are the people who believe that their ideas are simply the best. They're not here to engage in collaborative idea-generation, but rather to foist their pre-conceived ideas onto everyone else. Which means they bring a judgemental and decisive mindset to the table, rather than a respectful and open one. Not helpful for the generative, creative process! Confront bullies about their behaviour. Sometimes, they're not even aware that they are doing it! If all else fails, remove bullies from the group. No matter how great their ideas are, the cost to the project will be too high.

Remember: decision making and judgement comes at a later stage. Generate the ideas first; you don't have to execute any of them!

Environment

Photo: Levi Szekeres

The environment in which you work has a big influence on your ability to be creative. Faced with the choice of building an environment that's conducive to creativity or not – well, it's pretty much a no-brainer, although when you look around at some of the workplaces today, it makes you wonder. The good news is, it's possible to design an environment that is more conducive to creativity.

When we say environment, we don't just mean the physical environment. Many organisations make the mistake of thinking that setting up a creative environment just means painting the walls in eye-wateringly bright colours. Or buying some funky furniture and cool toys. These are but a part of the total environment – and actually a relatively minor one at that. If you're fortunate enough to be in a position to make some modifications to your physical environment, by all means, be our guest. Use it as a team-building opportunity. You'll have some fun!

Thing is, the psychological environment is actually much more important in terms of fostering creativity. And it's much harder to get right, because it's more or less invisible. The good news is, cobbling together a psychological environment that's conducive to generating Olympic-class creativity costs virtually nothing. It just takes patience and the right attitude. No budgetary approval required!

Treat your team (and yourself) with empathy, kindness and respect. Give everyone permission to play, to explore, and most importantly, to fail. Show everyone that it's okay to take things apart, and to question everything.

Get the environmental conditions between your ears right, and you have the power and flexibility of being a creative force to be reckoned with pretty much anywhere you find yourself, 24/7!

Models and best practices

There are heaps of models and methods for getting creative. From de Bono to Michael Morgan to Mark Victor Hansen.

Photo: Filipe Frade

Take the time to read up on these techniques. They all have something interesting to say, and provide plenty to think about, particularly if you're new to creative thinking, and want some help in setting up base-camp. Have a look at as much as possible of what's available out there, and decide which approaches work for you.

Beware the inherent danger with these models and methodologies though. If you're not careful, you could fall into the well-worn trap of thinking that merely perusing this material will make you creative. Many organisations spend thousands of dollars putting their executives through creativity workshops where they learn all the latest techniques but emerge with nothing much more than a glazed and dishevelled look to show for it. If you don't have the underlying attitude, not to mention a little aptitude, to be creative and innovative, simply

We've found these simple techniques useful: interrupting the train of thought with something ridiculous, rephrasing the challenge, and drawing parallels with something utterly unrelated.

going through the motions of these methodologies will be a waste of everyone's time. Buying a guitar and enrolling in Clapton's master-class won't make you musical if you can't tell a g-string from a crotchet.

Sources and non-sources of ideas

Conventional, passive and external sources of ideas such as committees, focus groups, customer surveys, and trend analysis can only go so far. Here are some less obvious sources for ideas that you may not have thought of before.

Do heed your annoyances

When something is annoying you, it can be the seed for great new ideas, motivated by a desire to remove the annoyance. Annoyance indicates the potential for new possibilities.

What are some of the things that annoy you about your work, your industry, your community and your life? What is it exactly about these things that annoys you? What could be done to fix them or make them better?

The next time something pisses you off, don't just get annoyed – get even. By using your annoyance as a springboard for new ideas.

Some of the world's best ideas have their origins in annoyance: When Ian Kiernan got pissed off with the rubbish he encountered as he sailed the oceans of the world in his yacht 'Spirit of Sydney', he instigated Clean Up Sydney Harbour Day on his return, which led to the birth of Clean Up Australia Day. And when Anita Roddick got angry at how big business treated third world producers, she started the ethical trade of natural products that became The Body Shop.

Photo: Lotus Head

Do tap into your passions

What is it in life that truly excites you? What enjoyable things or experiences do you spend your money on? If you could do just one thing every day, what would that be?

Many great ideas have come from individuals looking for ways to do more of the stuff they love doing. How can you turn your passion, or a facet of your passion, into a project or a job? Can you bring part of your passion to your work? How?

When Paul Cave looked up at the Sydney Harbour Bridge and thought: wow – wouldn't it be exciting to climb that – BridgeClimb was born. Snowboarding combines passions for surfing, skateboarding and skiing, and windsurfing/ boardsailing combines passions for surfing and sailing. Cow banks have proved to be a remarkable way to help people in developing countries break free from the cycle of poverty.

Tapping into your passions can also mean indulging in silliness, whimsy and fun! Think cult cartoons like Ren and Stimpy, and South Park. Think Pet Rocks, Tamagotchis, Frisbees and Hula Hoops.

Do listen to your intuition

In a world dominated by numbers, we often fall into the trap of over-analysis, and placing too much emphasis on pure logic, to the point where we forget, or suppress, our intuition.

In a world of constant and rapid change, numbers can really only show what happened in the past. Sure, there are loads of special tools and formulas we can use in an attempt to predict the future based on past numbers, but these are still only guesses, even if they are reasonably well-educated!

Rather than just relying on the numbers to make decisions, also listen to your gut-feel. The numbers may have come from the best experts, but your gut-feel is intimately connected with who you are and what you're about, and that's worth a lot.

And if you find yourself in a situation where you're faced with a choice between gut feeling and numbers, go the gut!

Don't follow fashion

Just because everyone is doing something doesn't necessarily mean you should follow suit! Fashion is not originality. Fashion is mass conformance.

Seek surpetition through design. Create something unprecedented for your organisation. Have a design philosophy. Your design should be a reflection of *your* tastes, not those of the market.

"I never get the accountants in before I start up a business. It's done on gut feeling, especially if I can see that they are taking the mickey out of the consumer."

Richard Branson

Gut feel decisions are more likely to lead to the creation of something new and unexpected. Reacting to numbers usually means you will be following an established trend.

Don't blindly react to customers

Sure, customers are a great source of ideas – after all, they're the ultimate test pilots. But there's always a danger in taking customer surveys relating to product satisfaction too seriously at the innovation stage. Do involve customers in product improvement, partner with them to make something better, involve and engage them in the process. But beware of letting them direct your decisions on new, ground-breaking ideas – they may not have the visionary big picture viewpoint necessary to see the real longer-term potential of these ideas.

Customer surveys on brand new ideas may work against innovation because customers on the whole are reactive. They're used to choosing from what's put in front of them, and great at imagining how to make the existing offerings better. Ground-breaking products and services have almost always come from organisations pursuing innovation regardless of what customers thought they wanted. How customers reacted to a previous product may not be that relevant to a ground-breaking concept!

For example – when the Aeron chair was first created, customer focus groups consistently gave it extremely negative feedback. But once people started sitting in the chairs, it became a hot seller, and a status icon. Similarly, if Google had used customer surveys to inform the design of their homepage, we almost certainly wouldn't have the elegant simplicity that has become a stand-out trademark.

Who directs your design flavour – you, your design agency, or your consumers?

Hip fashionistas, style slaves, runway divas chic websites and slick ads move aside for Feral Cheryl.

Feral Cheryl is the Aussie Anti-Barbie doll. This is no ultrafashion doll with freakish proportions and tortured feet. Feral Cheryl is a real wild child from the rainforest region of New South Wales, Australia, "Unlike other 'fashion dolls,' Feral Cheryl is *not* blonde, and not ridiculously thin. She goes barefoot, has tattoos, dreadlocks, simple clothes, and a handmade rainbow bag. She lives simply and with a healthy body shape, and pubic hair... (hmmm, maybe more than we wanted to know). Feral Cheryl has no fashion wardrobe, sports car, wedding dress, beauty shop, *or* holiday camper.

www.feralcheryl.com.au

> **Instead of asking customers what they think of a brand new never-before-seen product or service, ask them to tell you all the different ways they use your existing product or service. This may lead to great ideas for improvement. Your customers as a group will know your product or service more intimately than you could ever hope to – and you'd probably be more than a little surprised if you knew how creative they were in finding uses for your products!**

Customers would have wanted links galore. And finally, it wasn't a customer who thought up the idea for Post-It notes at 3M. It was one of their employees, Spence Silver, who was working on something completely different at the time. And incidentally, it took another employee, Art Fry, to figure out what to do with it – the teamwork thing. The rest, as they say, is history.

Evaluating ideas

How do you work out if an idea is worthy of your energy and passion? Whereas generation of ideas is all about playing without judgement, idea evaluation requires some level of rational decision-making and judgement.

First, draw up a set of judgement criteria. What are the outcomes that you want? What does success look, smell and feel like? What resources are available? How much time have you got? What are the realistic potential barriers to your success? Who can you call on for help? Now assess your ideas against these criteria.

Ordinary projects vs innovative projects:

Ordinary projects are ones that are necessary and important from an operations viewpoint, like finding a new information system to manage your inventory. Innovative projects will set your team or your organisation apart from the others. How many ordinary vs innovative projects are you currently working on? Your challenge: Can you turn an ordinary project into an innovative one?

Photo: Davide Guglielmo

The ease with which an idea can be sold to a conservative Board is often a useful indicator. The harder an idea is to sell to the Board, the more valuable (from an innovation viewpoint) it could be!

Don't forget to listen to your gut. Which ideas feel right? Which of the ideas excites you the most?

Full-steam ahead!

Once you've made a decision, be careful about falling back into idea-generation mode. This can lead to 'never-ending creativity' syndrome, where nothing is ever decided or put into action. Now, we're all for idea generation, and there's always a better idea out there somewhere. But the thing about being an intrapreneur is that you actually do things with ideas. There comes a time when you need to draw a line and get yours happening and out there! (There comes a time when we need to stop writing this book and get it printed!)

Selling ideas

If you're truly passionate about what you do, the selling process will take care of itself. You don't need to be an 'expert salesperson' to get results.

People are generally put off by cheesy sales pitches and formulaic tactics. We all know them when we hear or see them, and we cringe at the thought of being 'sold to'. When our turn comes to try to sell, this is the perception of 'sales' that we hold, and so we baulk at the prospect, but feel that we have no choice.

So how do you get people to buy your products, services or ideas without engaging in the stereotypical act of 'selling'?

You simply need to align your passion with what you're doing – and selling. Passion provides an innately truthful enthusiasm which attracts people like a magnet. If you have passion for what you do, people perceive you as genuine.

If it's your genuine intention to contribute to the world through your project, people will sense it, and embrace your ideas. No pushy selling required!

The perils of failure – and of success

Current business practice doesn't put enough emphasis on taking risks, experimenting, and celebrating failures.

As a society, we molly-coddle our kids – to their ultimate disadvantage. What's the use of going through school and not experiencing failure at all? It's time for a reality check. Pull up a chair and listen closely. We can't all be good at everything. Too harsh? Welcome to the real world. We should applaud those who excel in particular fields, and gently but firmly tell those who aren't cutting it that they too are on this planet for a reason, but this particular discipline obviously isn't it.

We need to respect and celebrate brave failures. It's through failure that we make our most valuable discoveries, and hence our most significant progress. Use failures as lessons – that's what they're for. Pioneering = failures! You can't have one without the other. They'd still be looking for Australia if a certain navigator hadn't lost the plot way back when. If you don't take the opportunity to get out of your comfort zone, you'll never learn anything, and never achieve anything.

Look at the greatest entrepreneurs and survivors. Most have overcome adversity and received their education at the school of hard knocks. You can learn a little bit from the mistakes of others, but it's your own mistakes that provide the learning that sticks. Failure makes you more resilient and tenacious.

What is failure anyway? Hint – it's all about attitude, confidence, accepting yourself warts-and-all, and being able to laugh at yourself.

Not being scared to fail sets those who accomplish things apart from those who don't.

But wait, success isn't necessarily all good either! Easy initial success can result in complacency, arrogance, stagnation, or unrealistic expectations for future projects. If you don't know why you were successful, you're not going to know which bits can be used on other projects. Alternatively, you might decide you're a genius, and can do no wrong. That can get ugly.

!

WARNING
DULL
COMFORT

Source photo: Salvador Barbera

When was your last (spectacular) failure? Shift your thinking!

When was the last time you had a spectacular success, and it held you back?

Kate Bezar

Founder of *Dumbo feather, pass it on.*

In my former life, I used to be one of those 'short term, cost-cutting management consultants' that Zern and Lisa refer to so endearingly in the first chapter.

I wish there'd been a book like *Cubicle Commando* back then because I couldn't see any way to be true to myself within the organisation I worked for, and so out of desperation and frustration, I became an entrepreneur. Many times since, I've longed for the resources I had access to back then, the team of brilliant people I had around me, and the kind of freedom that came from knowing there was a pay cheque at the end of each week. I came to realize that I'd taken a lot for granted.

You may have heard that saying about consultants – that they'll borrow your watch to tell you the time. Consultants are smart. The first thing we'd do when we went into an organization was interview people at all levels. We knew that they already knew what needed to be done to fix what was wrong, or improve on what was already there. That's where the saying comes from, and that's where intrapreneurs come in.

When I left consulting, I started a publication called *Dumbo feather*. Each quarterly issue profiles individuals who are living their passion with creativity, integrity and an entrepreneurial attitude.

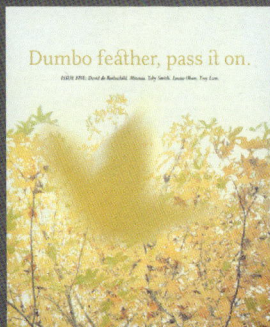

Dumbo feather, pass it on.

(some of) Abi's artists

always.
already

Images courtesy of Dumbo feather

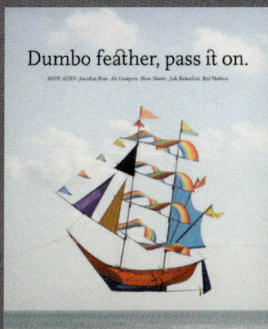

As editor, it's my job to get inside these people's heads, to understand their journey, where their ideas come from, and where they source their inspiration. Somewhat ironically, my life's come full circle, and I'm now being asked by corporations to consult to them again. Except now I help them to foster an entrepreneurial attitude and encourage innovation amongst their people. Now I bring to them the lessons I've gleaned from the people I've profiled and from my own journey. Here are ten lessons from just two such people: Abi Crompton (*Dumbo feather Issue* 7) had a degree in Fine Arts, but had always been frustrated by the elitism associated with most art and galleries. One day her father, a linen importer, bought too many tea towels of the wrong colour and size. **[Lesson 1: embrace accidents/stuff ups]** He asked Abi if she wanted them. **[Lesson 2: say 'yes']** It got her thinking… **[Lesson 3: dream more]** What if she commissioned artists to create works to be printed onto tea towels in limited edition? **[Lesson 4: Look at old things in a new way]** Here was a way to take the elitism out of art and bring it into the everyday. **[Lesson 5: find your cause]** The resulting business, Third Drawer Down, is booming, and has since expanded into napkins, 'artkerchiefs', table runners, and more. Fairly quickly, Abi learned from feedback that people weren't using their tea towels to dry dishes, but instead wanted to put them on their walls. Framing was expensive, blu-tac unreliable, and drawing pins left holes. So she invented Magnart **[Lesson 6: don't compromise, invent]**, a magnetic

hanging device which has much broader applications than just displaying tea towels.

Toby Smith (*Dumbo feather Issue 5*) was a law drop-out with a passion for coffee back in the days when it was tough to get a decent brew anywhere outside Italy. **[Lesson 7: find your passion]** After a stint in South America, Toby returned to Australia and started roasting in his mother's back yard. **[Lesson 8: start small]** Soon most of the neighbourhood was popping round for coffee under the washing line and buying his beans, but Toby was faced with a dilemma. With a very limited budget and firmly entrenched competition like Lavazza and Belaroma, how could he get cafés to use his beans? **[Lesson 9: embrace constraints]** Toby decided to start teaching café staff (the name 'barista' was unheard of back then) and consumers what really good coffee should taste like. **[Lesson 5: find your cause]** He also educated people as to where coffee comes from, and the benefits of Fairtrade. Toby's Estate is now incredibly successful, and supplies many cafés around Australia with their beans. **[Lesson 10: A good short black will get you a long way]**

www.dumbofeather.com

Photo: Amy Piesse

Photo: John Curnow

Never

never, never, give up!

never, never let fear steal your dreams.

Photo: Zern Liew

6. Systems

The case for rules and processes

Surprise! Systemised processes do serve a valid purpose.

They're not all bad: there's a genuine need for efficiency and consistency within operations. Without them, there would be repeated mistakes, debilitating inefficiency and, potentially, total chaos.

The industrial revolution was largely about systemising the means of production in order to maximise efficiency, and therefore profitability. Technology has enabled organisations to achieve unprecedented automation and standardisation of processes, bringing powerful leverage.

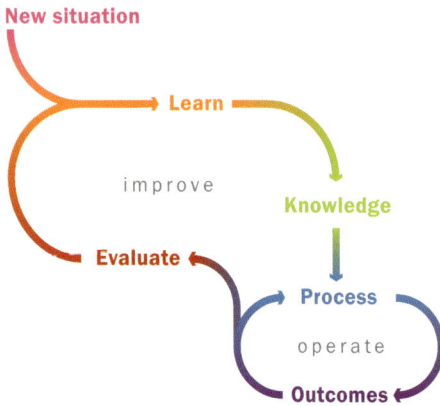

New situation

Learn

improve

Knowledge

Evaluate

Process

operate

Outcomes

Organisations are becoming increasingly complex, often developing and maintaining huge networks of global inter-connections. The ongoing challenge is to master rapidly changing and emerging industries in the context of various cultures, societies and governments. This requires enormous vision, and intellectual acuity and agility. Valuable lessons are learnt every day. Systems make it possible to capture and codify the learning, enabling the desired processes to be replicated consistently.

It's important not to let the means become the end. Just because complex systems have been put in place to deliver today's solutions doesn't mean that we should descend into serving these systems as ends in themselves. Systems are supposed to help us achieve our desired outcomes. We should be absolutely prepared to turn them upside-down, to challenge, dismantle and rebuild new systems to create new outcomes.

As an intrapreneur you're able to engage with systems and processes from several perspectives. As a person working to turn your ideas into reality, it's inevitable that you're going to be working within and around systems to get things done. As a revolutionary, you need to

Agility and adaptability are major challenges for businesses right now.

How to maintain the advantages of systemisation, but make everything flexible enough to enable faster response time to changes? How to speed up the learn-evaluate-improve cycle?

decide which established systems to challenge, and when. As a process designer, you need to be aware of the importance of systems, and to consciously design and

In recent times, there's been an increasing focus on the relevance and importance of systems thinking, which acknowledges the fact that nothing operates in isolation. Systems are there to be leveraged – for your innovative projects!

implement systems that work consistently, but have sufficient flexibility to enable innovation.

The paradox of process and innovation

Systemised processes are, by their very nature, anti-creative. They're about consistency, repeatability, and minimising variations. They're about not having to think too much.

On the other hand, creativity, which underlies innovation, is all about encouraging the unexpected, about originality, about looking for exceptions. It's about actively questioning and challenging, about making mistakes, and about thinking.

This often presents a paradoxical challenge to organisations that are trying to become more innovative. To be innovative requires re-invention, and doing new things. Fear of the new is compounded by having to significantly change, or even discard, stable processes that may have taken decades and a whole lot of money to put in place and fine-tune.

Photo: Andrew Eldridge

A process is a predictable, consistent reliable engine. Innovation is a massive upgrade to that engine.

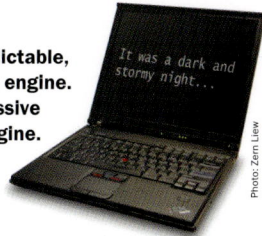

It was a dark and stormy night...

Photo: Zern Liew

In terms of management thinking, innovation is a relatively new concept. For many decades, management has been thinking with the mindset of a factory when designing systems and processes. Innovation on the other hand has happened more or less on an ad-hoc basis, and has invariably been driven by entrepreneurs, people who were forced to become 'outsiders' because they refused to play the game of conventional management thinking. Think Richard Branson (Virgin), Anita Roddick (The Body Shop), Steve Jobs (Apple), and Ricardo Semler (Semco).

And here's another paradox. With innovation becoming increasingly critical for survival and growth, it's imperative that organisations establish processes to enable them to innovate! In other words, organisations now need stable processes to practice disruptive re-invention. You, the intrapreneur, have a lead role to play in this emerging trend.

Systemising innovation

Organisations can't operate efficiently without systemised processes. Nor can they survive and grow without innovation. So as an intrapreneur, you need to provide leadership in creating a process that encourages and supports innovation.

Creating an 'anti-process' process

By definition, a process for innovation is a process designed to short-circuit and interrupt other processes, in order to enable innovative changes to be introduced. An innovation process is, fundamentally, an 'anti-process' process!

You probably already have an in-built process for innovation – you just haven't formalised it yet. If you're a naturally creative person, you'll be looking around you and asking 'why?', 'how?' and 'why not?'. A formal innovation process does just that. It allows, indeed forces, your organisation to stop and ask 'why?', 'how?' and 'why not?' at regular intervals.

An innovation process doesn't have to be a big-bang approach. Indeed it's probably wise to avoid regular total upheaval. The interruptions caused by the innovation process should be as brief as possible, providing time for people to stop and think. And they need to deliver clear benefits, not ongoing chaos, otherwise there's a fair chance you won't be invited back.

It's wise to take things one step at a time. Think big, but start small with little experimental innovations. Move forward incrementally, and make sure you've got something worthwhile to show for your efforts at each stage of the process. Maybe you can convince the Board to let you operate a little idea-incubator. They're unlikely to let you bet the farm, which is understandable. Make inroads by tinkering on the edges. After all, that's often where some of the most exciting stuff happens.

What a nightmare this whole innovation business is – we like the systems how they are. Why change things?

A real change for the better can bring freshness, excitement and the potential for freedom from old ways that no longer serve anyone.

Photos: Rachel Fuller

Bureaucracy, and the inevitable red tape that accompanies it, tends to grow when processes become ends in themselves. Rules and regulations are embraced to such an extent that they take on a life of their own and become counter-productive.

The original goals and desired outcomes that were the reason for establishing the process in the first place can go missing in action. The danger increases as roles become increasingly specialised, and the wider goals of the organisation are lost due to an inability to retain a vision of the bigger picture.

Working the system (or not!)

Leaving to start up on your own is always an option for the free-thinking innovator, which is great if that's what truly excites you.

Before you do that though, why not consider harnessing all the power and resources you have available to you in your organisation right now to do great things from within? This is an opportunity well-worth exploring.

Let's face it – big organisations are backed by huge resources, and wield enormous influence. So doesn't it make sense to do everything in our power to make sure that influence is shaped in positive ways, towards building a better future?

For example if you work for a bank, and can see opportunities for innovation, sure, you can go out on your own. Fact is though, you'll probably find it much easier to leverage the resources of the organisation to help you realise your dreams. Use your passion and vision to prod the sleeping giant into action, and make a huge difference without leaving your day job. After all, creativity and invention is all about re-configuring existing components in new and exciting ways.

Working the system is a mindset shift. It's a different way of perceiving organisational bureaucracy. You need to find a balance between accepting and challenging the established ways of doing things.

PROD

Photo: Tijmen van Dobbenburgh

The good news is, more and more organisations are realising the need to give their employees opportunities to challenge, explore, create and innovate, and to be themselves. But don't just sit around waiting for opportunities to arrive at a cubicle near you – make them happen. Today!

Embrace constraints

This is about embracing the challenge of working within real-world constraints. Constraints are not necessarily bad, and can actually make it easier to proceed.

When you embark on a new project, knowing the constraints – those things you cannot change – forces you to establish some parameters. These can serve to inform and guide your subsequent decisions, without necessarily being constrictive.

Having said that, be careful when accepting these constraints. Are you sure they're not actually fears that you could and should address? Is it worth challenging these constraints?

Be open to reviewing the constraints you have identified as the project proceeds. Nothing is forever. Things do change.

Always look to leverage each constraint. Inspiration and opportunity are often found in the most unlikely places. Such as between a rock and a hard place!

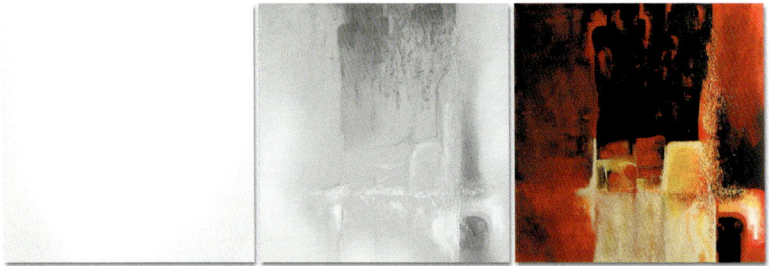

"As an amateur abstract painter, I often find a blank canvas very daunting to contemplate. By literally 'dirtying' the canvas first, I often find it easier to start work. The final painting emerges from the initial dirtying marks." Zern

Leveraging systems

Think of systems and processes as tools to help you work towards, and achieve, your goals.

It's about getting the establishment to work for you, rather than fighting against it. If you find yourself being swept downstream by a raging torrent, it's no use trying to swim against it. The trick is to go with the flow, letting its momentum carry you along as you search for opportunities to extricate yourself.

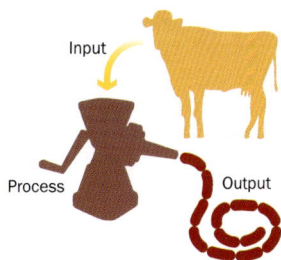

Input

Process

Output

In simple terms, a system is a set of inputs, processes, and outputs.

We're often told that something can't be done, and it can be tempting to believe it when everyone around you is saying so, and has been saying it for years, or even decades.

The mainstream publishing industry is a bit of an antiquated sausage factory – one size fits all, with one main distribution channel. We realised that there were a whole lot of other ways to publish and distribute books, and we intend to really shake things up. Watch this space!

For centuries, women were told that they couldn't be doctors, dentists, scientists, engineers, truck drivers and so on. Whoever would have thought that Annika Sorenstam would have been teeing it up in a men's PGA tour event?

The thing is, systems can often be leveraged to a far greater extent than we realise. The key is to shift our perception. To use a system to your advantage means first knowing what you want, i.e. the outputs that are the aims of your projects. Then you need to know what processes are available to assist in achieving those outputs, and what inputs those processes require to make that happen.

Knowing what you want

It's important to define what you want very clearly. If you're headed nowhere in particular, chances are you'll get there. It's a good idea to write your goals down so you can refer to them regularly. It's amazing how the act of writing something down can crystallise your thoughts and focus your energy. This also avoids the potential distraction of forgetting what it is that you're trying to achieve when you're busy running around trying to identify the systems and points of leverage that could work to your advantage.

Having established your big-picture goal, the next task is to break it down into smaller steps. This makes it easier to identify particular systems that can help in achieving one or more of those smaller targets.

Systems are generally designed with a view to specialisation, simplification, and compartmentalisation, so it's unlikely that any single one of them will be useful for anything more than a small part of your project.

If you don't make your own plans, you'll probably become part of someone else's, and chances are they won't have much of a role for you.

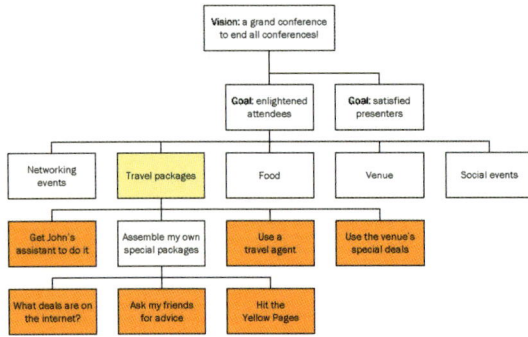

Vision: a grand conference to end all conferences!

Goal: enlightened attendees

Goal: satisfied presenters

Networking events

Travel packages

Food

Venue

Social events

Get John's assistant to do it

Assemble my own special packages

Use a travel agent

Use the venue's special deals

What deals are on the internet?

Ask my friends for advice

Hit the Yellow Pages

Example

The orange boxes are the systems that you can leverage to help you to achieve one of your goals, which ultimately contributes to the realisation of your vision.

Vision ➡️ Simpler Goals ➡️ What systems can you leverage?

Knowing what systems are out there

It's important to learn about the systems around you. Be curious about how things work. Always be asking questions, even, no especially, about those systems that may at first glance appear to be outside the scope of your project. Your desired output may rely on several different systems concurrently, or involve various systems sequentially.

It's often enlightening to look at the original reasons behind the systems that are currently in place. Try to understand why they were established, and under what conditions. Do those conditions still apply? If they're still relevant, are your requirements in defiance of these conditions, or do they acknowledge them? This arms you with valuable contextual knowledge with which to challenge these systems if necessary. If your project actually supports and furthers the aims of the system, you'll find it much easier to convince those who are part of the system to work for you – maybe even breaking their own rules – because they can see that the eventual outcome is in alignment with, rather than a threat to, their goals.

Exercise: What are the different systems out there you can leverage to get this?

Systems = people

Always remember that you're working with people. Everyone wants to be listened to, respected and valued, but individuals have different drivers, needs, intentions and baggage; and they're not always rational.

Aim to get on the good side of people where possible. Start with the intention of engaging positively with everyone you encounter. Be passionate about what you're trying to achieve, show them how it can make their lives better, and ask for their input! Respect their position, and work hard to show them the real value of your innovation. You may find that you can inspire someone who originally threatened to pole-axe your project to become your ally, helping you to circumvent long-standing rules rather than using them against you. Outcomes like this make it all worthwhile.

Don't forget, sometimes a system can be encompassed within a single individual.

Different paths to the same end

Use systems to your advantage, or be used! Systems are only means to ends. If a particular system or combination of systems proves too hard to navigate, pick another combination. Change course. There are many ways to skin a cat. Try another way.

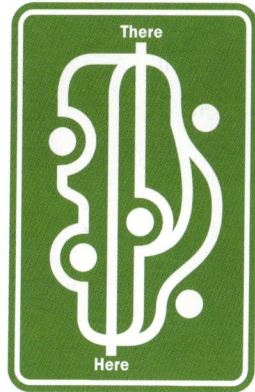

Be careful when choosing the systems that you think will help you to achieve your goals. Try to work with the prevailing systems wherever possible, and only go against the grain if you truly believe it will significantly benefit your project. Avoid alienating people who are part of prevailing systems just to make a petty point, or flouting the rules simply because you don't agree with them, or don't like the person who is enforcing them.

Identify systems that could work for you (the good roads), and those that could work against you (the bumpy roads). Become the friend of both. Listen especially closely to those people working within the systems that could work against you, as their insights can provide key points of leverage. In addition, develop contingency plans in relation to those systems that could work against your project. If you know there's a muddy patch ahead, what can you do now to prepare yourself for the possible loss of traction when you get there?

Rule-breaking 101

Rule-breaking is part and parcel of the exciting life of an intrapreneur. Effective rule-breaking is an art well worth learning. As with all decision-making, you need to do your homework and be very clear on the cost-benefit analysis of any actions that will break the rules. Make sure they're worth breaking.

When doing a cost-benefit analysis, the most important costs and benefits are usually the non-monetary ones. Have you sometimes found yourself wasting energy (or even angst) on an issue in an attempt to gain a small monetary advantage, only to discover it's not really worth it in the end?

Often, the cost is not as high as you might think. Although large organisations tend to be inordinately fear-driven (duh!), the reality is, people don't get fired all that often for rocking the boat. They might become victims of a widespread slash-and-burn cost-cutting

Sometimes it is better to do something first, then apologise for it later, if required! Apologising afterwards rather than stopping to ask for permission up front can be really useful at times.

exercise, but that's a story for another day. Usually, temporary annoyance from your boss or the board is about as bad as it gets. This will, of course, be mitigated in the fullness of time by the results of your dazzlingly innovative project!

Pick your battles.

Picking the right battles requires clarity of purpose. You need to have a cause, a grand vision, and to be consistently true to your values. Do you really need the benefits that winning this particular skirmish will bring? Can you let this one slide, and find other ways to win the war?

Limiting Rule:	Liberating Idea:
You need to get accepted by a publisher to write and publish a book.	I can self-publish!
But self-publishing is a really expensive process.	I'll find a way to under-write the costs up front!
I don't have the time to write, publish and market my book.	I'll assemble a team of people to help me!
Self-publishing means you can't get a publisher to back you.	Self-publishing means you have full creative freedom to innovate beyond the boring conventions.

But everything is working so well. The economy is booming, trade is through the roof. We're meeting our sales targets, and we're growing. Why change something that isn't broken?

You need to be constantly changing, and searching for new opportunities. You have to be out there, everywhere, all the time. Take an honest, holistic, integrated approach to business and to life. Look at the big picture. Leverage existing relationships, strategic alliances, collaborations. Adopt an abundance mentality.

It's all very well to try and turn things upside down, but how will people know what's happening, and who's going to answer to the Board? I think we should set up a committee to look into it.

There's always a way to fast-track things – learn the systems, find the KPPs (key pressure points), persuade the right people, show them the benefits, and make it happen. If the powers-that-be are made to realise that their endless 'due-diligence' processes are stifling innovation and actually increasing risk – the risk of falling off the back of the bus – sooner or later they're going to have to change, or be left behind.

Photos: Rachel Fuller

The resistance

There are a number of obstacles that can threaten to prevent you from adopting and living the life of an intrapreneur in your organisation:

Complacency

Change is exciting. It's a breath of fresh air, an opportunity to blow away any stagnation. Mediocrity and sameness have been done to death. They're *so* twentieth century. Let's do something different, something better. Right now!

Bureaucracy and red tape

Some organisations can be so risk-conscious that even the slightest move has to be ratified by a committee, and takes months to receive approval.

You're too young/inexperienced/low down in the org chart to introduce changes.

You're never too young or inexperienced – good ideas can come from anywhere – it's how you present them that matters – and we're here to help teach you that.

Of course I'm right – I've been doing it since you were in nappies. In any case, I'm only doing what my boss tells me to do, because it's not my job to challenge anything. Why rock the boat!

We just need to remain positive, and find ways to work the system and hit the buttons of the people with bad attitudes.

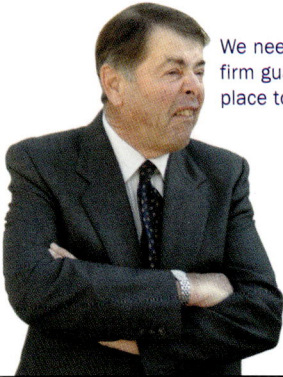

We need more analysis, more research. We need a firm guarantee of success – this isn't the time or place to be taking risks.

Be true to yourself, take a risk and continue to stand up for what you believe in. If you're constantly bopped on the head, maybe it's time for a change, but don't die wondering. Life's too short.

Despite occasional anecdotal reports to the contrary, management are people too! And being people, they're subject to the usual range of hopes, desires, aversions, and doubts. So engage their emotions, and get them excited about your project. Show them that their future depends on it. And make them smile.

Inexperience

Only the very arrogant or insecure believe that decisions have to be made at or near the top of the heap.

Experience can be useful if you have it. If not, what better way to gain experience than by taking action right now? If you never have a go, you'll never ever know!

And as for being but a humble functionary in the greater scheme of things, we suggest you consider the advice of the inimitable Anita Roddick – but you'll have to wait until Chapter 8.

"When the rate of change outside exceeds the rate of change inside, the end is in sight."

Jack Welch

Bad attitude

This is where the egos and agendas of management and/or the lassitude of 'drones' prevent new things from happening.

The trick is to discover their pain or fear, and then promote your project in a way that addresses their issues.

Fear

Often, the more senior or 'experienced' an employee is, the less inclined they are to take risks. They have reputations and fiefdoms to defend, not to mention a comfortable retirement beckoning, so long as they don't rock the boat.

Some people accumulate 30 years of diverse experience. Others simply repeat what they learned in their first year on the job 30 times.

Fail fast, fail cheap, and fail often. You're going to make mistakes – no question about it. It's the only way to find out what works and what doesn't. Treat mistakes like you treat luck. Both are necessary, arrive when they're least expected, and add to the fun of the journey.

Accepting the things you cannot change

While we think it's a rarity, and don't for a minute suggest throwing in the towel until you've exhausted all possibilities, some things just aren't meant to be.

It's great to hold on to your vision and dreams, but always remember that there are many paths to the mountain top. This may mean that sometimes you need to get off the track you're on and scramble through prickly bush for a bit, and sometimes you may even have to back-track a little. Or stop for a breather.

Accept that some changes can take a long time. And that some things are just too hard to change. We often get so excited about our ideas that we forget that other people may not see things exactly as we see them, or feel such a sense of exhilaration and urgency. We forget that some changes are not possible or feasible, given our situation. It's important not to become impatient, nor to waste time and energy torturing ourselves.

When things genuinely become all too hard, be kind to yourself, and let it go.

If it all gets too hard, and you really think leaving is the right path for you, Robert Gerrish and Sam Leader of flyingsolo.com.au offer loads of resources and motivation to strike out on your own.

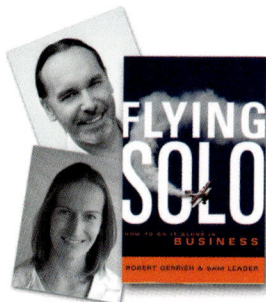

Seek the serenity…
to accept the things you cannot change,
the courage to change the things you can,
and the wisdom to know the difference.

So easy to say, so hard to achieve;
and so absolutely worth your while learning to do!

Photo: Zern Liew

Remember, you can always get takeaway!

When the systems around you just won't support your vision of a wonderful home cooked meal (the fridge broke, the food spoilt, there's no power, the shops are shut, you have no kind neighbours who'd lend you anything); look wider afield – get takeaway!

Takeaways in real life: Apple uses Intel chips in their computers. L'Oreal leverages The Body Shop's ethical pedigree to bring soul into their business. Your local telcos all share the same network infrastructure.

Photo: Zern Liew

Systems further afield

So what should you do if, no matter what you do, you simply cannot get your idea to take flight? If the systems around you can't deliver what you need, are there systems further afield that could serve you? What potential is lurking within other areas of your organisation? Have you scanned all levels of the hierarchy for opportunities?

How about opportunities to work with other organisations? Inter-organisational collaboration is gaining traction as a way of combining the resources, systems, and thinking of separate groups to achieve synergy and mutual competitive advantage. Is it time to forge new alliances with an external partner or a competitor? At first, this may frighten the horses, but as in all your intrapreneurial endeavours, it's all about the potential long-term benefits.

When all else fails, you may need to look at massive systemic change on a personal level – and jump ship! Maybe your ideas just need a whole new environment, offering different contexts and applications, to enable them to come to fruition.

Beware of conventional change-management. The way it's done now often leaves a lot to be desired. Go for involvement, not enforced changes. Yes, this takes time and effort. But it is worth doing.

Involvement

Whenever you do something new, be it implementing new systems in search of innovative outcomes, re-thinking how your organisation approaches challenges, or starting a cool project, there's likely to be some pretty serious change happening. Everyone needs to feel part of the adventure. The more they feel ownership, the more they'll rise to the challenge. A well-planned and executed involvement strategy is a necessary part of your change-management process.

The key to obtaining involvement and engagement is to create a system that listens to, and then actively implements, suggestions wherever possible. Once again, we're working with the fundamental human need to be heard, acknowledged and valued. There's nothing more demoralising than the ubiquitous suggestion box that seems to lead directly to the Bermuda Triangle.

Genuine idea-generating and actioning systems can yield invaluable outcomes and mind-shifts, while also serving to motivate the organisation. If everyone in the organisation feels involved in the innovation process, potential enmities are diffused, and the possibility for creativity increases exponentially.

Other ideas

So, having confirmed that the best way to maximise the creative potential within any organisation is to enable everyone to become involved in the quest for innovation, how can that be achieved?

Start an 'Intrapreneur Club'. Invite fellow intrapreneurs (from either your own or other organisations), indeed anyone with an idea to float (and if you've been paying attention, you'll know that means every-one), to come together to share ideas and support each other's cool projects.

The importance of saying NO. As an ideas, creative person it's very easy to see the potential in every-one's projects and be tempted to get involved. You need to cultivate an awareness of what's on your plate and how much you can offer, so you can say no if neces-sary. Resist the temptation!

This will not only help your growth as an intrapreneur, but also help showcase your organisation as one of the most switched-on outfits around town, a handy advan-tage in the increasingly competitive battle to recruit and retain the best minds. This should be a good enough reason to hit your boss for some resources to help establish your Club!

Similarly, why not start an 'Intrapreneur Workshop' to help and encourage intrapreneurs to develop prototypes and new systems.

It would be good to involve someone in your Club or Workshop who's across all the innovative projects that are happening, both within the organisation and, as much as possible, around the world. This would have the duel benefit of avoiding duplication of ideas, and assisting people to make connections and work collaboratively with like minds.

There are also many virtual systems available that can help your organisation to centralise and share ideas, and to bring people together from disparate geographical locales to brainstorm and troubleshoot.

Develop an 'Ideas Register' or 'Cool Projects Register' so that anyone in the organisation is able to locate projects that excite them, and get involved. This needs to be backed up by an organisational culture that encourages and supports people's involvement in innovative projects. That, of course, may need a little work to establish.

How about an 'Innovators Exchange' program, whereby organisations identify their brightest intrapreneurs and arrange temporary placements in another organisation (which may not even be in the same industry)? In return, they host an innovator from another organisation for an agreed term.

Sidetracked by the change train

> If you're spending too much time working against the system, perhaps you need to call on your mentor. He/she may be able to pull those strings and make life that much easier.
>
> Spending all your time fighting a system can be a real waste of energy, and if done to excess will exhaust you and your team. Ask for help. Or find another way.

Sometimes, in the course of leveraging a system to your innovative ends, you find that you need to make changes, despite having no intention of doing so at the outset. This can be a good, or a not-so-good, thing.

It's important to understand that when you're on a roll doing exciting things, there's always a danger of getting sidetracked and heading off into another project (or projects) altogether.

You need to draw clear boundaries so that it's easy to identify what's actually part of your project, and what's out of scope. That's not to say you close your mind to all new ideas and possibilities that occur in the course of your project. Never stop being open to possibility, but understand that as an intrapreneur, you need to deliver results; otherwise you'll find your stream of party invitations drying up remarkably quickly.

Sometimes you may have to head down a sidetrack and take on a secondary change project in order to clear the way for your main project to proceed. It's quite okay to do this, so long as you're very clear on why you're doing it, and on where the boundaries and expectations of this detour lie. Never lose sight of the big picture.

IBM Australia

Having had many years of working on many great
projects with IBM, here are my observations of
how IBM fosters and works with intrapreneurs.

Zern Liew

Engaging Intrapreneurs

By empowering people to implement their own ideas and providing them with the
support to put these ideas into action, IBM fosters an environment that is conducive to creative problem-solving and engaged involvement; and consequently
innovation.

IBM also provides employees with comprehensive tools and resources on innovation, including podcasts, presentations, initiatives, offerings and success stories.
Employees are encouraged to join communities of practice where they can
collaborate with other employees with a similar set of expertise, interest, and
passion for a particular area. Technology like TeamRooms and teleconferences are
used ubiquitously to keep ideas and communications flowing between teams that
are often spread across geographical divides. There are virtual spaces where
employees around the world are encouraged to submit their ideas and thoughts on
specific problems. There are also on-going competitions to encourage innovative
thinking.

IBM's management model is about trust, support and encouragement. Employees
are encouraged to take ownership of projects, and are given authority to make
decisions relating to those projects. Employees are empowered to run with their
ideas, mostly with minimal bureaucracy. There are systems and controls in place of
course, as is necessary with an organisation of this size and breath. The good thing
is, IBM intrapreneurs on the whole are able to innovate within these systems
successfully.

Rewarding Innovation

There are of course a whole set of awards that recognise innovation and the creation of new patentable concepts.

To really help create an environment that fosters creativity and innovation, leaders must encourage and support innovation. To this end, IBM leaders – senior executives to team leads – have 'innovation' written into their measurements.

IBM employees themselves also have a mechanism to recognise other employees who have helped them with their work. This encourages collaboration and teaming.

Diversity is the key

Compared to most other organisations, IBM is incredibly diverse in so many aspects of its operations. It employs people from diverse backgrounds; it engages in R&D, and services clients across diverse industries and sectors. It is the enthusiastic and active embracing and leveraging of this knowledge and human resource diversity that makes IBM stand out, and provides great fuel for the continuous creativity so essential for innovation.

Intrapreneurs are the key to innovation within corporations like IBM.

IBM is one of the largest R&D spenders in the world, resulting in lots of new concepts, and new patents annually. IBM is committed to innovation with their current 'What Makes You Special?' innovation drive (http://ibm.com/au/innovation).

7. Rewards

Photo: Sanja Gjenero

Photo: Zern Liew

Success — what's your *definition?*

"Until you value yourself, you won't value your time. Until you value your time, you will not do anything with it."

M. Scott Peck

Valuing yourself and your contributions

So why do you bother doing what you do? Sure, you're driven by a need to make a difference, to live by your values and to stretch yourself. To learn, discover, explore and create. To engage, motivate and enable others. You also work hard for your organisation, and in the process contribute momentous value to its well-being and profitability.

You absolutely deserve to be rewarded for that! People are the heart and soul of every organisation, and intrapreneurs like you who go way beyond the call of duty to ensure that the organisation not only survives, but thrives, deserve to be recognised and rewarded.

Many intrapreneurs we've met seem to share a common trait of not being able to see the true value they bring to their organisations. Intrapreneurs are so good at generating new ideas and making cool projects happen that we often forget that we are extraordinary!

If you're not used to doing it, learning to value your contributions can take some time, but it's well worth doing. In order to ask for, and receive, the rewards you deserve, first you need to know what you're worth.

Once you've determined your true value, get very good at asking for, and politely persisting until you receive, what you're worth. Many people live with the false but enduring hope that their managers will experience an epiphany, suddenly realising their true worth to the organisation, and showering them with hitherto unimagined wealth. Unfortunately, this very rarely happens. That's why you need to get good at asking for what you want.

Photo: Kevin Garcia

Knowing what you want

What do you want by way of rewards? Is it recognition, promotion, early retirement, increased responsibility, new challenges, or just cold, hard cash? As an intrapreneur, it's likely that you'll be looking in large part for intrinsic rewards, but at the end of the day, as noted way back when, money does indeed make the world go round.

So what *do* you want? This is a creative challenge with a difference – one that you apply to

What do you want?

yourself. It's time to turn your creative prowess inward, and to concentrate on envisioning exactly what you want from life.

Rewards to support your life

Start by writing or drawing a detailed description of what your ideal life would look like. Put in as much detail as you can. The more detail you include, the more you have to work with.

Now determine what aspects of that vision you can conceivably satisfy through your work. Money is definitely part of the reward package, but explore the wider possibilities. Can you design a package of rewards, bearing in mind the realities faced by your organisation, that will help you join the dots of your ideal life picture?

Photo: Katinka Kober

Show me the money

Okay, let's talk money. Money is obviously a big factor when you're working for an organisation. There are many ways of getting paid, and there's always room for negotiation.

There are three basic ways to work for an employer:

1. Under an Award – currently 80% of workers are covered by an award – these set a minimum hourly rate of pay, plus other entitlements such as holidays, sick leave and super payments. Technically, you can negotiate anything above the award rate.

2. Under an Enterprise Agreement – minimum rates of pay for ordinary hours and annual leave and sick leave are regulated, but everything else is up for grabs. This gives you a lot of flexibility – for example you could arrange to work a set number of hours over a year, with flexibility in choosing when you work them. This is the 'annualised hours' approach.

3. Under Contract – Increasingly common as companies try to reduce their overheads. Essentially, you agree to work for a set term for a set rate of pay. Paid leave and super are not automatically taken into account under these agreements.

Some tips on negotiating your salary:

• Put yourself in a position where you are indispensable to your employer.

• Never be the first to mention a salary figure

• Do some homework on what you have achieved for the company so far – how much you've saved them, how much you've made for them, and other non-monetary benefits you've provided.

• Also, work out how much you want, but more importantly need, from them.

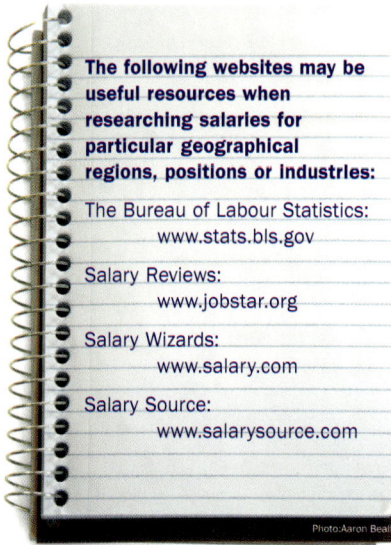

The following websites may be useful resources when researching salaries for particular geographical regions, positions or industries:

The Bureau of Labour Statistics:
   www.stats.bls.gov

Salary Reviews:
   www.jobstar.org

Salary Wizards:
   www.salary.com

Salary Source:
   www.salarysource.com

Photo:Aaron Beall

Some salary comparisons are useful as a benchmark – but only as a benchmark. You're worth what you're worth, and this book is all about not limiting yourself and your beliefs by following the herd.

Show me some other stuff

Other things to ask for, instead of, or in addition to, the folding stuff are: salary packaging, e.g. additional superannuation contributions; fringe benefits such as education, training, seminars and work-shops; a car; child care; low interest loans; profit-sharing schemes; flexible working hours and conditions, including telecommuting; and additional leave to pursue personal interests (which will of course make you more creative!)

Sit down and brainstorm some cool possibilities!

Intrinsic rewards

For work to be truly meaningful, it's necessary to also consider an entirely separate category of rewards. This is the area of intrinsic rewards, and includes such things as satisfaction, a sense of contribution, of making a difference, and of empowering, supporting and helping others.

Everyone has their own list of intrinsic needs. What are yours?

Creative rewards

Gift vouchers (www.lastminute.com.au)

Pay an employee's mortgage for a month

Pay for a house-cleaning service

Monthly massage (www.3minuteangels.com)

Tickets to concerts, ballet, theatre, sporting events, etc. (www.ticketek.com.au)

RedBalloon Days (www.corporate.redballoon.com.au)

Shopping cart spree (give employees 10 mins to throw whatever they can into a trolley)

Fridays off in June

Customised books (www.messengermarketing.com.au)

Salary packaging possibilities

RDOs, flexi-time, work from home, duvet days, parental leave, extra day for each year of service

Overseas conferences

Industry memberships

Further education

Additional superannuation

Personal Mentor/Life coach program

Shares in the company

Travel passes

Corporate club (e.g., American Club) memberships

Mortgage payments

Car payments for spouse or partner

TV, DVD, electronic goods

First class air travel upgrades

Paid week at Christmas time

Home computer

Salary sacrifice for charity

Lunchtimes reading to disadvantaged kids

Believe in yourself and your value.
Be passionate about the product –
you!

Asking for what you want

Once you know what you're worth, what you want, and how you want it, it's time to ask for it. This is all about convincing your boss and your team of your worth to the organisation. It's about selling yourself to them. Remember the key to successful selling in Chapter 5? That's right – passion. If you're not genuinely passionate about your true value, then Houston, we appear to have a problem. You should expect to be paid a decent, fair amount of money for your efforts! We often undervalue ourselves, and therefore sell ourselves short.

Prepare a cool presentation which demonstrates how your innovative performance has helped the organisation. When preparing this document, include the objectives of the organisation, how you've helped them towards achieving those objectives (list everything you've done, highlighting any major achievements), and how much money you've saved or generated for the organisation. If you're currently getting paid $60k and last year you saved the organisation $500k, make sure they're aware of that.

Some of the savings and revenue that you've facilitated may be a little difficult to quantify. How much are those creative strategic alliances, community partnerships and philanthropic collaborations you initiated really worth? Who knows, but they're definitely worth something, so include an estimate.

Sad but true

It's frustrating that many people who don't have particularly good ideas or skills continue to get ahead primarily because they're shameless, and persistent, in asking!

You do often get what you ask for!

What is it that you bring to the organisation beyond your technical skills and work experience?

Do you motivate and inspire your colleagues? Are you great at jumping in and getting your hands dirty to fix a problem? Are you a calming influence in stressful situations? Do you ask good, insightful questions?

Photo: Davide Guglielmo

At the very least, whoever reads your document should be extraordinarily impressed that you've shown initiative and taken the time to review and document your achievements. Include the challenges you've faced, and list the lessons you've learnt. Also list your 'wow' failures! Don't get too ambitious though, and have some sound reasoning to support your estimates. It's difficult to sign bonus cheques when you're laughing so hard you've got tears in your eyes!

It's important to stick to your guns. Assuming you haven't got a little ahead of yourself and your assessments and requests are reasonable, you need to maintain a confidently assertive approach. Don't fold at the first sign of resistance, but on the other hand maintain a sense of reason and reflection to ensure that you don't inadvertently wander into a parallel universe where arrogance and aggression is the order of the day. Not nice.

While it's generally true that if you don't ask you don't get, asking does not automatically mean that you will always get. But it's a start. And if you still don't get, maybe it's them that don't get it, and it could be time to ask elsewhere.

Photo: Bianca de Blok

"I'm being exploited!" Leave.

Branding yourself

The world is changing fast, and we have to work harder and harder, or smarter, to stay ahead of the game. There's really no such thing as a secure job, or a fixed position description or job function you can lock down tightly any more. We're already changing careers seven times on average over the course of our working lives, and many of the jobs we'll do before we shuffle off to the great innovation lab in the sky are yet to be invented. Life-long learning and continual innovation is the catch-cry.

The world of work is a highly competitive marketplace, and part of valuing yourself is to start thinking of yourself as a brand. As a brand, you become more saleable – to your current organisation, to other organisations, and to the public, should you decide to strike out on your own. Your brand is vitally important, because it encompasses the whole you. When you live and breathe your brand (i.e. when you're true to yourself), it helps to keep you real.

The key questions to ask yourself are 'What am I telling my (internal and external) customers?', 'Why do I do what I do?', and 'How can I do it better?'

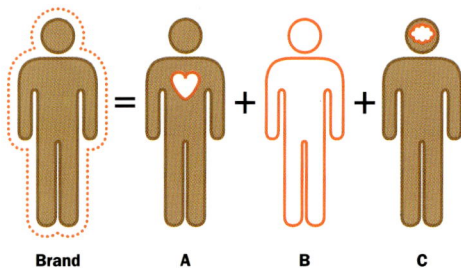

Brand   **A**   **B**   **C**

A values + ethics + beliefs + vision + promises + integrity
B how you dress + speak + act
C your saleable skills + knowledge + experience

A does not really change. These elements are core to your being, and failing to acknowledge them will leave you unhappy and unfulfilled. Living and working in such a way that you honour and remain true to them will ensure that you lead a rich and rewarding life.

B is changeable. As you grow, and become more aware of who you truly are, these facets will change to align with, and more accurately reflect, the elements in A. You become more integrated and real. Just like an organisation's brand, your brand needs to be authentic and consistent.

The days of thinking of yourself merely as a performer of a specific job function are over. Separate your true self – who you are at the very core of your being – from what it is that you do. **C** is where all the benefits of lifelong learning and experience accumulate.

In the beginning, your brand will be what you say it is. Over time, it will become what others say it is, so take every opportunity to educate others about your brand. Your visual brand is the first experience customers will have of you, so make sure it clearly represents the essence of who you are. Be consistent and true in what you wear, and in what you say about yourself.

Bangalore

Sadly, when we think of CVs and job-hunting (or even setting up a business of our own), we generally only think of C. But this is the easiest part to replicate. It's a commodity! Remember the trend towards offshore outsourcing of white-collar jobs that was unimaginable just a few years ago that we talked about earlier? Without an identifiable brand, something that articulates the unique values and talents that you're able to offer, you run the risk of remaining 'that person in accounting'. And becoming 'that person in accounting whose job we outsourced to Bangalore for a quarter of the cost'.

Selling yourself to the world

The world is indeed your oyster, cup cake, chow mein, borsch, lamb tangine, babaganoush… whatever. But you need to think global, and act personal.

Acting personal means networking, making connections, and building relationships. Full bandwidth. Totally present, body and soul. No cutting corners and being half-there or half-baked.

Given that, despite the ever-changing wonders of technology, we're increasingly time-poor, and our to-do lists continue to overwhelm us, it's often tempting to avoid meeting people in person, opting instead for 'more efficient' methods such as phone and email. And because most people are doing this is precisely why you should be doing exactly the opposite!

Yes, it takes time and effort. Effective selling necessitates building authentic emotional connections with people. To do so requires investing time in getting to know people – what makes them tick, what they care passionately about. It's about genuine relationships, not the number of names in your little black book.

So who are you having coffee with today?

Photo: Jean Scheijen

Networking

Networking is a seriously under-rated tool. It has the great advantage of being about as personal as you can get without attracting the attention of security.

It's important to look beyond your team and your immediate circle of contacts in order to sell your brand to the world.

Cultivate really broad and diverse networks, and make sure they always spiral outwards, as opposed to looping back in on themselves. Network within your industry to keep abreast of developments, and for support, but also go further afield, to where the people you will eventually impact are. Form strategic alliances with like-minded businesses and competitors – see opportunities everywhere.

Attend some networking events regularly, but also tap into other groups occasionally, e.g. you might go to Last Thursday Club every month, but Women's Network Australia once every six months.

Build fabulous advocates – third party endorsement is so much stronger than you banging on about how good you are. You want others who really believe in you and your project to be out there talking about you all the time. Then you need to be out there everywhere to back it up. If you give out referrals, you will receive referrals, so be out there selling others as well – they'll appreciate the help, and will reciprocate.

Photo: Stefano Barni

Networking is all about getting out there and meeting new people. Is your networking in loopback mode? Imagine you're starting out as a party-plan consultant: your best friend agrees to host the first party with nine guests, but if the guests then take it in turns to play host, and the same group turns up each time, the networking situation is effectively in loop-back mode. You've still only met ten people. But if each of the nine guests at the first party hosts parties with nine new guests, who then each host parties with nine new guests, you've met over 800 new people, and are now in a position to meet a further 7,000 people... that's networking!

132 : Cubicle Commando

But I'm the shy type! I'm terrified of the concept of networking! I'm too much of an introvert. Learn to be comfortable meeting people. It's absolutely possible if you take it one step at a time. Start with changing your self-belief from 'I am shy' to one that is more open to meeting new people, such as 'I am okay with meeting new people one-on-one, in fact I quite enjoy it.' Move out of your comfort zone. As hard as it can be, try to sit with people you haven't met before. Appear confident – fake it 'til you make it! Walk up and introduce yourself to people – remember, everyone's in the same boat. To interest people, you have to be interesting! Learn to become a good storyteller. Be memorable!

Make connections from the heart! – talk to people because you want to – not for what they can immediately do for you. Don't bang on to people about what your project is about, but rather what it can specifically do for them, or people they know – focus on solutions, and how you can help solve their problems. Remember, networking is about creating valuable and lasting business relationships.

Believe in abundance and reciprocity! What goes around comes around. What you give out comes back ten-fold. Ask not what they can do for you, but what you can do for them. Want to know something? It's true. All of it! Remember, it's all about personal contact. Send hand-written thank you notes to let people know they're appreciated.

> Don't forget your friends and their friends! Simply having fun socialising is another avenue to meet new people (no, we're not advocating a mercenary multi-level marketing approach). Meeting new people in a non-business context can free us from our organisational straight-jackets, and re-invigorate our sense of community with others.

Great networkers have no fear of competition. They believe that there are abundant opportunities for everyone, in fact they believe that the more connections they make, even between third parties without necessarily getting involved themselves, the bigger the cake becomes for everyone. When you give with a positive attitude and no expectation of anything in return, somehow it just happens that you receive more in return than you could ever imagine.

Be proud of, and honour the value that you bring to the world. Be open to, and embrace, any opportunities that come your way. And be proactive about getting out there and meeting new people. They'll be so glad you did!

Last tip   it's so much easier when you're consistently true to your values, not driven by self-interest, and genuine in your aims.

Profile building ideas

You may not realise it, but you're always building your profile. Every decision you make, how you dress, your grooming, how you treat people, how you engage with work colleagues and clients, how punctual you are, how often and how big you smile and laugh, all contributes to building your profile. Is there anything you need to be working on?

Profile building is marketing for your brand. Consider being more proactive and targeted in your approach. After all, it's the most important campaign you're ever going to work on!

Some food for thought: when you engage with work colleagues and clients, what do you do that makes you unique? Do you write articles or record interviews for your organisation's newsletter, website, blog or intranet? Do you engage in debates with people on professional-interest discussion boards, or in public forums? Do you write articles or letters for publication in magazines, newspapers, or on the web?

Be out there everywhere!

Perception builds success, and success builds more success!

Other ways of building your profile include creating strategic alliances with your peers in other organisations, writing informative articles, getting involved in community causes and events, making the effort to meet people for no other reason than that you want to meet them, introducing yourself to and congratulating people you admire, accepting speaking engagements, mentoring and being mentored, and nominating yourself for awards. Just on this last point – it's not a sign of arrogance, and never get hung-up about winning. It's all about the journey, stretching yourself, and meeting awesome and inspiring people.

So, what makes you unique?
What does your personal brand stand for?
Who do you know now?
Who can you meet tomorrow?

Remember:

To love others requires that you love yourself first. To value others, first you must learn to value yourself.

Seeking your just rewards is about valuing your contribution. It's your responsibility to yourself and your wellbeing to look out for number one. So ask to be valued and respected.

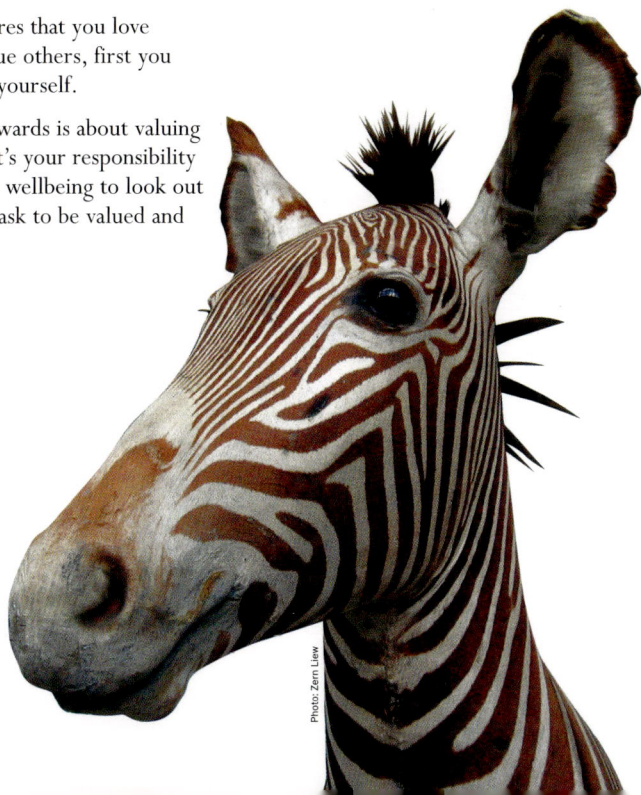

Photo: Zern Liew

Belinda Yabsley
Manager, Mercedes-Benz Airport Express, Sydney

The current business landscape is in danger of permanent stagnation. The majority of businesses are incapable of responding to change, embracing new thought principles, and acting in a new, inspiring, and visionary manner. There are many 'soldiers' working on the inside, battling for change, yet the resistance is strong – and territorial.

Businesses that are breaking new ground, and are therefore at the forefront of the future of business, are those that have looked seriously at the changing landscape of society. In observing how it is evolving, they have embraced diversity of thought, innovation as a foundation global attitudes to sharing, networking experiences, opportunities and information.

Innovation begins with an attitude and a willingness to embrace the unknown. When an organisation embraces innovation and evolves its traditional approaches, new channels of business emerge, delivering new financial and business development opportunities.

One of the most critical issues facing organisations today is that of employee engagement and retention. Those that have realised this are working hard to change their management, HR, and indeed their entire business if necessary to accommodate the intrapreneurial individuals within their organisations in order to reap the rewards.

It is essential to acknowledge your intrapreneurs for their individual styles and contributions, and to provide them with a career path to enable them to flourish, grow as people, and feel appreciated, appropriately rewarded, and empowered.

At Mercedes Benz, first we identify these people, and their unique skill sets. We provide an appropriate reward and recognition process, embrace their differences, and develop the culture within the organisation to acknowledge them. We then challenge them by giving them the freedom to explore and manage innovative new

business opportunities. We give them a lot of breathing space, coupled with appropriate responsibility and accountability.

Humanising the workplace is essential to achieving employee engagement. If you are asking more and more of your people, and want their undivided loyalty, enthusiasm and engagement, you need to create an atmosphere that inspires them to get out of bed and look forward to coming to work every day.

As you mature, you learn from your experiences, your mistakes, and from the people you have met. When trying to carve your path in the world, and within the organisation you work for, it is your necessary responsibility to communicate your objectives, work collectively with all members of your team, management and support staff and to empower those around you to understand your *modis operandi,* and in turn, champion your objectives.

The biggest mistake younger members of an organisation can make is to maintain an air of arrogance, ignoring the potential input those around them can provide towards achieving their objectives. You can be truly intrapreneurial within an organisation without being arrogant or aggressive. This takes a level of humility, maturity and wisdom where you are prepared to both learn from those who can teach you, and to inspire those who can learn from you.

Abacus Recruitment Solutions

Toby Marshall, Director

Innovation is our purpose at Abacus. It involves 90% of our time and resources. We work with smart organisations, helping them change who they hire and how they hire. We get our leverage from joint ventures and strategic alliances. Our role with all our external partners is as the innovator, the bringer of new ideas and new approaches to the market place.

There are a number of ways that we foster innovation to create new business ideas:

We surround ourselves with great mentors whom we retain and consult with monthly. All our mentors have very different expertise, and together they provide us with enormous insights and understanding.

We connect to the networks of our mentors. While the mentors themselves are inspiring in their knowledge of their particular areas, this is perhaps a third of the value they provide to us. By going to our mentors' public events, we get to meet their other clients – some of the smartest and most innovative people in this country.

We hire university and school students to work with us part-time in areas they know a lot about. For example in IT and marketing, we focus on leading-edge web and email marketing – the whole world of direct response sales and community building. Who better than these bright YOUNG people to create leading-edge technology. They live with this stuff every day that old farts over 40 don't even know exists!

We atttend heaps of conferences and read, read, read. Both on the web and books. How else do you learn anything? Watching Big Brother?

Finally and most importantly, we seek out and link with mavericks – those wonderfully exciting and creative people who see the world very differently. They could be anywhere! For example, some of my best insights come from a ferry skipper whom I ride with most mornings. If you only talk to people at your golf club, as so many senior business people do, is it any wonder they haven't had a new idea in their lives?

www.abacusrecruit.com.au

Thought Leaders
Matt Church, Founder and CEO

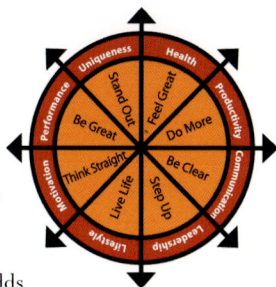

The concept of people being entrepreneurial within large organisations seems contradictory at first. If you see an organisation as a hierarchal, command and control, process-driven culture, then for sure, these ideas are at odds.

To be an employer of choice, a future-proofed, take-over-the-world business, you need diverse, lateral-thinking, results-focused individuals who respond rapidly to changing needs, and are fundamentally driven by the value required by the market, versus the short-term value to the shareholders.

Entrepreneurs organise teams of talented individuals to achieve specific, market-driven projects. When they fail, they fail fast. When they win, they win big, and everyone gets to share in the spoils.

Organisations are increasingly expecting people to do more with less, and as a consequence they will need to become more results-centred.

If you can get the job done in half the time, you shouldn't be punished by being given more to do, you should be rewarded by being given more choice – more choice in where you work, how you work, and what you work on.

The intrepreneur is driven by choice. Freedom is your battle cry, and results are your trophies. Cut the red tape, get out of my way, and don't put me in the same room as security-conscious, fear-driven dead wood who simply want to turn up and turn off.

I love what I do, and want to work with cool people on interesting projects that are successful, and are something that I can be proud of.

Matt has been an infopreneur for over 15 years. He is in the top 10 conference speakers in Australia and has authored 5 books to date. He is an expert at getting people clear on their master message.

www.thoughtleaders.com.au

3 Minute Angels
Andrew Ward, CEO

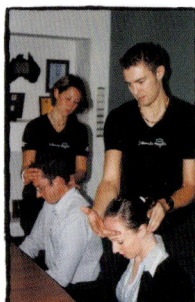

Things we do to foster creativity

We have an online Angel "university" which facilitates all the competency tests. Successful completion of the tests "ascends" the Angels and gives them better commissions. The company competencies fit criteria that accredits up to a year of study in a Diploma of Business Management.

We run regular market, territory and national competitions for the staff based on attitude and financial performance. Winners are acknowledged with everything from a round of applause to a 10-day trip to Melbourne and a ticket to one of the Melbourne Cup Carnival Race Days.

We use worksheets that allow the staff to talk about the job they have just done. Importantly, the worksheet seeks from the staff – "What was your best thing for the day" – this can be work or non-work related. It always supplies insight into staff morale for managers.

We have a common "knock-off" area that we use where everyone on a given night comes together and debriefs.

All our debriefs use the same format: "what was good" and "what was bad". IMPORTANTLY we ask that for each 'bad' the staff member identifies, they must offer a suggestion that could be carried out by them or the managers to address that 'bad'. Otherwise it is just bitching – and that takes no talent at all!

We have Angel of the month awards in each territory. Recipients gets to be the custodian of a trophy, a full body massage, and are placed on the website for time immemorial.

Andrew Ward, the CEO, has a standing offer with all staff to mentor them with any business ideas they come up with.

We have internally promoted 22 of our 24-person management team. Staff can see we put our money where our mouth is when it comes to career advancement.

3 Minute Angels has a staff of over 160 and outlets nationally. The company has pioneered many innovations in one of the oldest industries in the world: Massage. Our average age of the staff (Angels) is 22, and the management team has an average age of just 26. Despite this inexperience, the company has harnessed the entrepreneurship of its people to become the largest massage company in Australia. The company has sales of $2.5million per year and has grown at over 200% year-on-year since its inception in 2002

www.3minuteangels.com.au

ipac
Paul Gordon, National Strategy Manager

An intrapreneur's perspective

ipac decided to give me a go on MY terms. The result has been a successful four year relationship during which time I have assisted the firm to completely change their view on distribution. This truly bent ipac right out of shape, and created a point of difference in the marketplace, so much so that we do not have competitors, as our offer does not look like anything else in the market.

The lessons I've learned so far are:

(1) Trust in yourself. You must have faith that you can educate your internal corporate audience on the value of letting you fly.

(2) You must get results, but in the timeframe YOU predict, NOT an unrealistic timeframe set by the organisation.

(3) You WILL attract 'like' people around you who will enhance the proposition.

www.ipac.com.au

Liquidity Finance
Steve Fenton, General Manager

Encouraging creativity, intrapreneurship and personal growth

We put staff through a base self development curriculum and recommend staff undertake other development or studies – for approved courses we will pay 50% of the tuition. We hold a number of meditation meetings down on Balmoral Beach to put a creative tension in our business. We do quarterly marketing and visioning sessions on our personal and companies goals.

The by-product is: amazing people taking amazing steps; or people simply leaving. That's OK, everyone develops at their own pace. Maybe an idea won't flourish in your current environment. If so, it's up to the intrapreneur to find, or create, the right environment for their idea.

If we can understand the way that we create our own reality, we then have the choice to create what we want! We do not have to live by the mandates that society put on us – we can live by our own rules. That's a very nice kind of freedom.

Learn about what makes you happy, and be with people who make you feel good about yourself. Be a vital human being making a difference.

www.liquidityfinance.com.au

8. Impact

"If you think you're too small to have an impact, try going to bed with a mosquito."

Anita Roddick

Small cog, big impact!

Even the smallest component can make a huge difference. Think of the last time you had a great experience dealing with an organisation. The impact was made by the person with whom you interacted, right?

As a society, we tend to celebrate the big names, the high-profile people who head up organisations. Such is the way media has evolved – compelling, if somewhat air brushed, stories about larger-than-life characters. In reality though, it's the everyday people in organisations who make things happen. Indeed, without them, nothing much happens at all. And if they're not on the right page, all the publicity in the world for the celebrity CEO won't be enough to stop bad things happening.

You don't have to be rich and famous to start a revolution. Everything you do, every day, every choice you make, has an impact on the people around you. You can make a difference just by being you.

Being a mere cog in the machine has its advantages. You're not in the limelight, so you can operate under the radar, able to do your stuff without attracting too much

The further you are away from head office, the more opportunity you have to play, and to try new things. The closer you are to head office, the greater the pressure to conform.

attention from higher up. You can modify policies and sneak in subtle changes while still giving every indication of 'toeing the line'. This provides great opportunities to inject ideas and innovation into the organisation.

It's about consciously planning and focusing your actions in such ways that they make a disproportionately large impact – it's about leverage.

Photo: Claudia Cristina Mesa P

Your impact is wider than you think

Photo: Bo Hansen

Just as you are more than your job description, more than just an employee, the impact you have on the world is greater than you think. Your actions have an impact on yourself, your family and friends, your work colleagues, your organisation, your clients, your community, your country, and your planet.

In an age where communication technology is effectively shrinking the world, and where nothing happens in isolation, everything you do has the potential for unlimited influence, spreading outwards like the ripples from a stone dropped into a pond.

Identify opportunities to make an impact

Look at the things you're interested in, things that utilise your skills and stretch your mind. These may not necessarily be skills you're using in your current work!

Find learning opportunities – is there something you can do in an area of the organisation that you're interested in learning more about?

What are you passionate about? Can you find or create a project within your organisation that hooks into some of those passions?

Talk to your colleagues. Are they complaining about some aspect of their work that you may be able to change or improve? Talk to your boss. What is he/she grumbling about? Can you do something about it?

What are some of the difficulties you encounter in your own work? What can you do about them?

What are the stated goals and mission of your organisation? Can you initiate and lead a project that will make a radical contribution towards achieving those goals?

Photo: Zern Liew

An intrapreneur is a toolbox of amazing skills and experience. Your responsibility in life is to locate and eliminate problems, and to revolutionise the way things are done.

145

Measuring your impact

So how do you measure whether you've made an impact?

Before you get the tape measure and clip-board out, start by identifying, articulating and writing down what 'making an impact' means to you with respect to your current project. Remember to include the all-important emotional impact, the true value proposition of what you're trying to achieve.

Conventional measures

There are loads of these. Have you delivered the agreed outcomes? Have you met budget, and if not, have you performed commensurate with the organisation-wide blow-out? Did you meet the deadline? These are measures that everyone has to work to, but they don't tell the full story. And they're certainly not the source of innovation, or the 'wow' factor!

By all means document your performance in terms of these measures. Even if they don't add much value to the project, they might come in handy as 'hard' backup data when you're out there working the room. Always do what it takes to cover all bases.

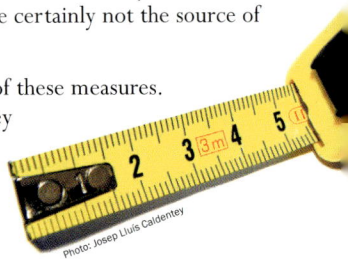

Photo: Josep Lluis Caldentey

Your emotional impact on others

Rather than concentrating solely on conventional statistical measures, it's important to also look at the emotional side of things. Innovation in business is about people, and people are creatures of emotion. Therein lies the best gauge for measuring the true extent of your impact.

Are you truly seeing and valuing what you do? Many creative people forget that what they take for granted – their talents, abilities, and insights – are actually quite rare and valuable things. Consequently, many simply fail to see the impact they have on others! To really measure your impact, you need to actually be open to seeing the value of what you do, and who you are. Ask close friends and colleagues to give you a detailed list of all the great things you've done, but may have forgotten about. You might be pleasantly surprised!

When you're making a positive impact, it will generally be reflected back to you in the behaviour of others. Take a look at the people around you. Do they seem happy to see and work with you? Do they give you genuine positive feedback? What sorts of things are they saying?

Sometimes we're so involved in what we're doing that we don't take time to step back and listen to feedback from the people with whom we interact.

If the people around you are genuinely open and supportive, it's fair to assume that you're doing something right, and having a positive emotional impact. If in doubt, ask someone you trust for their honest appraisal.

To ensure that you hear and understand the feedback accurately, learn to listen carefully. Take time to be genuinely interested in what other people are saying, and ask questions. Meditation can be immensely beneficial in helping to quieten your mind, enabling you to be more centred and in the moment.

Remember, this is not about trying to make everyone happy all of the time. Apart from being impossible, that won't help anyone, least of all you.

Monitoring your own emotions

Your own emotional state is a great indicator of the impact you're having on other people.
Learn to listen to your inner dialogue, and to observe your emotions frequently throughout each day.

Four quick ways to check how others are reacting to you:

Body language: crossed arms, body facing away from you are both not good.

Tone of voice: dismissive barks not good.

Language used: should be self-explanatory.

Length of conversation: lots of waffle or short sharp dismissive statements not good.

Photo: John Evans

Quickly check in on your emotional state when evaluating feedback from the world. Are you in an appropriate state to listen, evaluate and absorb? Too often we let our emotions overwhelm our ability to listen and learn, especially when faced with criticism. We can become defensive and protective in such situations, and that can stop us from listening. It's okay to say 'I'm feeling really bad now, but I want to hear what you have to say. Can we talk about this later, or can you put it in an email to me?'

What feelings do you experience when you're interacting with other people? Is it always the same, or do certain people and situations evoke specific feelings? Why do you think these situations or people elicit these feelings?

Look at the checklist above on evaluating how other people are reacting to you. Use the items on the checklist to monitor how you interact with others. Whereas it's next to impossible to change someone else, it is always possible to improve how you relate to others in terms of the items on the checklist.

Keep your body language open and relaxed. Practise thinking before you speak, so you have time to choose your words – we know this can be a challenge for passionate individuals! If you have a tendency to decide-and-run, make a point of hanging around for a few minutes and talking to people. If you get defensive easily, actively practise never crossing your arms, and always make your first response a genuine agreement with something they've said. It's amazing how these simple steps can change the way you relate to others, and help you to make a positive impact.

We each perceive a given situation in different ways. Our perception depends on the many factors (including our emotional maturity) that contribute to our unique personality. Sometimes a situation causes such a powerful emotional response within us that it becomes very difficult to perceive it rationally. Something may happen that causes us uncontrollable anger or debilitating depression.

When you're able to think clearly, it's worth writing down a concise description of the situation, and then doing a reality check. **Are your expectations of yourself or the world unrealistic?** Given the situation, are your feelings reasonable? Acknowledge you're feelings, know that things are not as bad as they seem, and will soon pass, and keep working in accordance with your values towards making an impact.

Expectations

It probably won't surprise you to hear that intrapreneurs like you generally have extraordinarily high expectations of yourself, the people you work with, and the impact of your projects. Let's get one thing straight – there's a fair chance that you'll never totally achieve your ultimate expectations! You need to aim

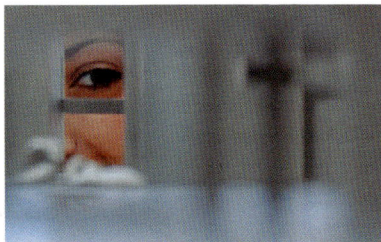

Photo: Sean Carpenter

as high as you can imagine, and accept the fact that you will probably never actually get there. This is the paradox of having grand dreams – and it's actually a good thing.

It's important that you set high yet realistic expectations, but these need to be consciously managed. Having inordinately high expectations without a corresponding degree of flexibility is generally a sure-fire way of setting yourself up for a fall. It's okay to have high expectations of yourself, as long as this is tempered with a high level of kindness. Beware the dangers of perfectionism.

Setting and managing expectations for others is more challenging. Generally, unless you know the people you're working with very well, it's better to set lower expectations than you would ideally like, and then work to facilitate over-achievement. This is a far more satisfactory and ultimately rewarding approach for all concerned.

Three things to remember about managing expectations: **(1)** Set lower, then over-deliver. **(2)** Don't commit to anything until you know the facts. **(3)** Listen to your gut feel and your heart – if something doesn't feel realistic, it probably isn't!

Technical expectations

At the outset, establish what's required in terms of tangible deliverables. Be clear on the budget, available resources, and time constraints, and on the required outcomes and deliverables. You need to meet these expectations in a measurable way. Meeting these expectations is not optional!

One cool way to get a sense of stakeholder expectations is by using the slider scales from *Radical Project Management*, Rob Thomsett, "Just Enough" series, Yourdon Press (Prentice Hall PTR), 2002, p.153. The scales can often reveal surprising and unexpected priorities of each member of the project team. The financial controller does sometimes value a quality outcome more so than saving money!

Emotional expectations

Emotional expectations fall into two broad categories:

External – those of others; your partner, family, friends, colleagues, clients. External expectations relate to those aspects of emotional intelligence that are to do with recognising emotions in others, and handling relationships in a positive manner.

External expectations

Internal expectations

Internal – your inner dialogue, in terms of self-image and expectations. Internal expectations are related to self-directed aspects of emotional intelligence – knowing and managing one's emotions, and self-motivation.

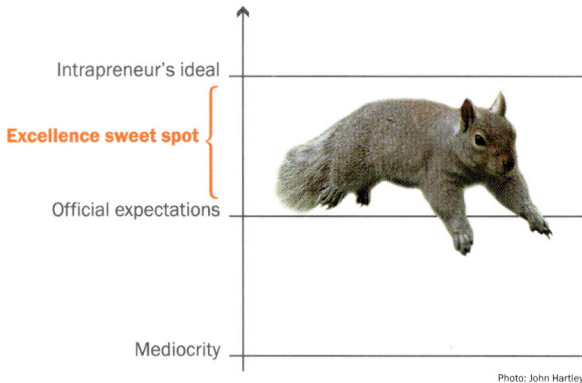

Intrapreneur's ideal

Excellence sweet spot

Official expectations

Mediocrity

Photo: John Hartley

A simple way to think about expectations

As an intrapreneur, and a champion of innovation and change, it's only natural to want to pursue excellence. This can be a problem when what constitutes 'excellence' is not clearly defined.

Try this approach. Identify the lowest common denominator (the mediocrity median?), and then determine your absolute intrapreneur's ideal. Somewhere above the common denominator, but nowhere near your ideal outcome, set your 'official' expectations. This represents an acceptable result, one with which everyone will be satisfied. Then you're free to go for gold. By achieving an outcome somewhere between the official or set expectations and your absolute ideal, you will have exceeded expectations – and achieved excellence!

Benchmark pitfalls

How you choose to measure your performance against others will affect the perceived impact that you have on your organisation, and on the world. There are several common benchmarking mistakes that can have a detrimental effect on your ability to innovate successfully.

Photo: Maxime Perron Caissy

Benchmarking by monetary terms

Yes, profits are essential for the survival and growth of every business, and so it's wise to be ever-conscious of your budget, and your performance in relation to it.

However there's a great danger in relying solely on monetary indicators. Obsessive focus on the bottom line can quickly lead to myopia, whereby the big picture, the vision and the cause sink quietly below the horizon. This makes about as much sense as totalling your Porsche because you took your eyes off the road to check out a 4-cents-a-litre fuel discount!

Think about the value your organisation brings to the world. If your organisation ceases to exist tomorrow, what would the world lose?

Instead, focus on the overall value your project will deliver to the organisation. If your project never happened, what would your organisation miss out on? Sometimes it's okay to go over budget if the ultimate value-add is worth it, but you need to have a strong body of evidence to support your case!

People only complain about money when the outcome is mediocre. In many cases, only the anal-retentive see saving money or meeting budget as an overriding success factor. What would you rather announce: "I've created amazing value and set the organisation up to kick butt", or "I've managed to come in under budget"?

Benchmarking by overly-simplistic measures

It's tempting to be sucked in by overly-simplistic measures. A good example is television ratings. What do these numbers mean, anyway?

If we use raw data as a way of interpreting complex processes like the impact of information delivery on society, we're in grave danger of ending up with a very warped view of the world. Worse still, this can become a self-perpetuating cycle. We become slaves to these scales, and lose focus on the greater impact of, and reasons for, our activities.

Benchmarking by established norms

Care needs to be exercised here, because established and accepted norms can and do change over time. 'Generally accepted' does not mean 'set-in-stone'!

People's size has changed over recent decades, with important implications for the clothing industry. Quality of finish and performance of cars has improved out of sight. What would have been considered optional extras only a few years ago is now considered an entry ticket only.

Sometimes, 'norms' turn out to be products of someone's over-active imagination. Take for example the 'standard' female figure used by fashion designers as the basis for their work. Notwithstanding the rare and wonderful creatures who prowl the catwalks at show-time, no

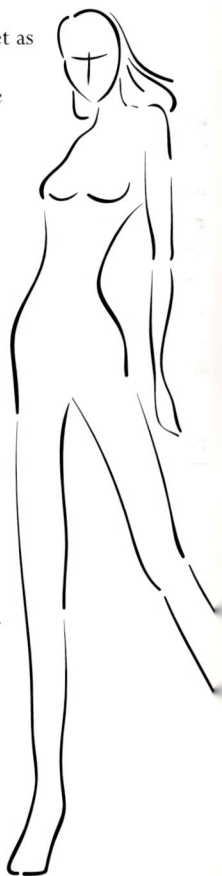

women actually look like that. How can we expect clothing that's designed for real women if designers are working to this flawed 'norm'?

Just because everyone expects something to be done in a certain way means you should avoid doing just that, if you want to make a real and lasting impact!

Benchmarking by others' expectations

This is about measuring your impact in terms of society's expectations, your partner's expectations, parental expectations, or any number of people not directly involved in your project.

At first glance, you may well think that these people couldn't possibly have that much influence on your work. Like it or not, the people who are closest to us have a significant subconscious influence on our performance. Many of us carry the expectations of our parents with us for much, if not all, of our lives. Sometimes we do things in an attempt to gain the approval of other people. Whose expectations are you measuring your impact against?

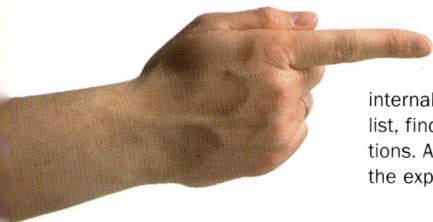

Sometimes it can be hard to differentiate between your true expectations and those you've internalised as a result of external pressures. Draw up a list, find some space, get calm, and review your expectations. Are they really yours, or are you merely channelling the expectations of others?

It's important to remain clear with regard to your expectations, and to constantly re-visit your cause and goals. Don't let other people's expectations overwhelm your focus. You can't please all of the people all of the time; and trying to do so will definitely prove counter-productive.

What does success mean to you?

So, what does success mean to you? Is it just about making an impact, or is there more to it?

Try an exercise in visualisation — describe what success looks like in your world. Draw or paint a picture, write a story or compose a song or a play, whatever enables you to get a clear sense of what this thing called success means to you.

Check in with your inner-self to make sure that your description of success is your truth, and not someone else's.

Set your description of success aside for a few days. When you return to it, does it still ring true? Can you expand on it? Are there aspects you need to change?

When you don't measure up

This happens sometimes. Such is life. Your intentions may have been honourable, all the hard work may have been done, but for one reason or another, things just didn't work out.

Photo: Vladimir Babich

Own up and take responsibility. There's nothing worse than running away from reality and ignoring the issue, or failing to take responsibility for your actions. Identify positive courses of action that are available to you, and get on with them.

It's easy to say and often so hard to do, but make a conscious decision to learn from each failure. If you never fail, you will never move forward!

Learn to forgive yourself, and to be kind to yourself. One failure does not necessarily mean bad outcomes forevermore.

A small list of reminders: be kind to yourself. Start a gratitude journal and write down the things you are truly grateful for each day. Keep your resumé up to date, and celebrate your achievements!

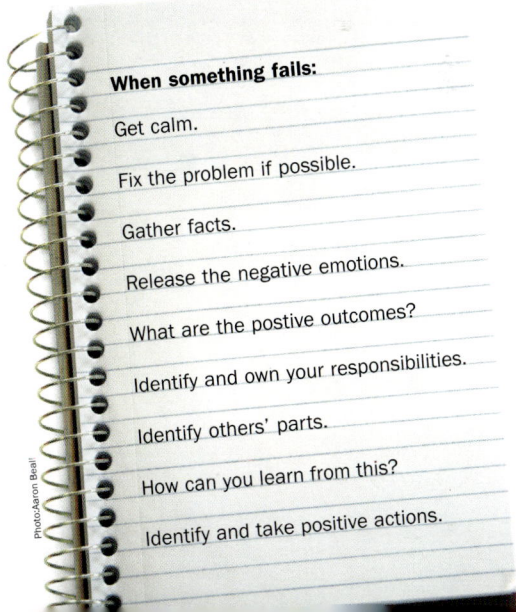

When something fails:

Get calm.

Fix the problem if possible.

Gather facts.

Release the negative emotions.

What are the positive outcomes?

Identify and own your responsibilities.

Identify others' parts.

How can you learn from this?

Identify and take positive actions.

Photo: Aaron Beall

Love Communications

My Main Philosophies

1. You are what you think about most of the day

I believe this is one of the greatest discoveries in history. We have been given control over one thing in the universe – our thoughts! Clearly, God sees this as important. If we choose to think positively and clearly, we can sculpt a great life. If we're negative and disorganised in our thinking, our results will mirror this.

2. The 80/20 Rule Rules

The 80/20 rule is profound. It says that 20% of what we do gives us 80% of our results. In other words, only a few things we do each day account for most of our success. The corollary of this is that most of what we do is close to useless! By spending more time every day on the vital few tasks we can revolutionise our lives and still get home to watch the News!

3. Sow First

Remember the old saying "You must sow before you reap"? It's a timeless adage and a true one. But most of us forget it. Many people want rewards first, they want something for nothing. But if we focus on giving instead of getting, then great results are assured. Eventually. Sowing the seeds of success is slow and time consuming, but it will eternally be the only way to create lasting success.

4. Be Clear

What are your goals today? This week? This month? This year? This decade? Most people have only a foggy idea at best. Clarity is power. When I'm super clear about where I'm going and what I need to do, I get big results first. When I'm muddled and not really sure about my To Do List, I get mediocre outcomes. That's why it's absolutely imperative to spend several hours each week focussing on where you want to go and what you want to be.

5. Choose to be Happy

Most people don't realise that happiness is a choice. Long term happiness, it's not really dependant on what happens to you, but rather your reaction to what happens. When we choose to be happy no matter what your current situation is, happiness manifests. When we wait for our life to be perfect before we are happy, we have a long wait indeed.

You don't need a reason to be happy. Just choose to be so, right now.

154 : Cubicle Commando

What would I say to an intrapreneur if I met one today

Remember everyone works for themselves. An intrapreneur is really a one-person business that just happens to be inside someone else's company. Run your business well!

Relationships count. Spend as much time having good human communications at work as you do on your daily tasks and success is assured.

Remember to learn. Spend 30 minutes a day studying your field and you will soon be a master of it. And masters get the big bucks.

It doesn't matter! Life is short, and nobody is likely to ever remember you or your company in 100 years. So chill out and have fun!

Siimon Reynolds is one of the most renowned names in the Australian marketing industry.

Siimon has won almost every major advertising award for creativity in the world, including the Gold Lion at Cannes, the Gold Pencil at the New York One Show and the Grand prize at the London International Advertising Festival.

In Australia he has won Newspaper Ad of the Year, TV Commercial of the Year, and Magazine Ad of the Year, and has won Advertising Agency Of The Year twice.

Siimon is a winner of the International Advertising Association Scholarship and NSW Young Achiever of the Year, career category.

He has lectured nationally on advertising to over 50,000 business people, and is a successful author in six countries.

5 ½ years ago Siimon co-founded Photon Group. In May 2004, Photon listed on the Australian Stock Exchange, and now has a valuation of around $230 m. Siimon remains one of the top 3 shareholders. Photon now consists of 23 marketing services companies, employing over 1000 full and part time staff.

Siimon is also Creative Director of Love, a fast growing branding, PR and advertising agency, a Director of the Sydney Film Festival and a published author in 8 countries.

9. Life

Intrapreneuring for your life

Intrapreneuring is as much about creating a meaningful life for yourself as it is about helping your organisation to become more competitive, profitable, and sustainable. Intrapreneuring is about bringing soul into the world of business.

To open and tap into the heart and soul of the organisation, first we must tap into our own true selves. It's important to recognise that organisations can be messy political and social beasts, however it's possible, indeed crucial, to bring your entire being to work. To be truly committed and fully productive, you need to be permitted the freedom to be yourself at work.

Organisations that encourage and support the presence of the whole person in the workplace are consistently recognised as great places to work. They benefit from higher levels of loyalty, commitment, productivity, and innovation, and lower levels of staff turnover and absences.

Such an environment can be threatening to the Garys of the world – those who are too frightened to change with the times.

"One of the things I learnt when I was negotiating was that until I changed myself, I could not change others."

Nelson Mandela

Why should I bother with innovation and making changes to the system? I do my job, they pay me. I'm happy – I think. I don't need this. Tell someone who cares!

You only get to experience a deep sense of fulfilment if you're prepared to take risks and follow something you truly believe in. Experiences and achievements are what make life amazing, not drifting along in a daze, doing the same things over and over again, and going nowhere.

Photos: Rache

People who refuse to change will eventually render themselves redundant. In today's increasingly chaotic and competitive world, the rules of the game are constantly being re-defined. Standing still is no longer an option. The more intrapreneurial you become, the more chance there is that you'll overtake your boss on the road to success, not to mention the road to knowing who you really are as an individual.

One thing's for sure – if you sit around waiting for conditions to be favourable, you'll miss the boat completely. If you're waiting for someone else (like your boss) to give you permission to be intrapreneurial, you're behind the eight-ball before you even begin. You have to grasp the bull by the horns, be willing to take some risks, and then push it to the limit in order to succeed!

It's an interesting truism that the dominant species in any system is always the slowest to change. Their dominance lulls them into a false sense of security, and they often become extinct before they realise what's happened.

Despite the inherent risk in being part of a vulnerable minority, stay passionate and dynamic, and don't be discouraged or slowed by those who have a vested interest in keeping things just as they've always been.

"The unexamined life is not worth living."
Socrates

Use your life experience and the challenges you encounter to grow and embrace your whole self – your values, your beliefs and your vision. Work is a large part of your life, therefore it's important to be totally aligned with what you're doing. You need to believe in your organisation, what it stands for, what it does, and where it's going.

Who are you?

Whenever you start a new project, you need to know the parameters within which you'll be working, the resources at your disposal, and the goals that you're working towards. It's the same with the most important project you'll ever undertake – your life. Start by working out who you are, what you're about, and where you're at right now. Analyse your strengths and weaknesses, and be very clear on what you want to achieve.

To make even the smallest change, you need to be aware of, and honest about, how things really are. It all starts with you – the inner you.

Dig Your Own Groove!

Goal: Fill your life with things that align with your values, and discard all things that don't. This will bring a profound sense of satisfaction, joy and deep meaning, with the result that you will value yourself so much more. Values triggers might be: freedom, adventure, learning, pleasure, winning, beauty, feelings, growth, optimism, discovery, understanding, relationships, leadership, spirituality, creativity, mastery, contributing, teaching, and sensitivity.

The six facets of you

When reviewing your life, it's useful to address six facets, each of which contributes to your overall well-being. You can then drill down into each area to build a more complete picture of your inner self:

Mind & body: Do you like yourself? Are you generally happy and optimistic? Do you have an open heart and an open mind? Do you have acceptance with regard to change and loss? How healthy are you? Do you make time to exercise regularly? Can you walk up a flight of stairs without panting? Do you eat well? Do you laugh a lot? In short, are you happy with your life?

How we feel about our lives can provide the motivation for change. This kind of honesty comes with a warning – it could seriously affect your life, and there's no turning back!

" *Of the multitude of questions that arise in a person's life, there is little doubt the most challenging one to find an answer for is, 'Who am I'? It is likely that throughout all of recorded history, this single question has at one point or another at least crossed the mind of virtually every human being that has ever lived. While some people do seek an answer to this important question, the reality is most choose to push it out of their minds, for the simple reason that the act of contemplating upon who they really are actually serves to make life even more complicated than it already is! This tendency on the part of mankind to live 'unexamined' lives is what the late Fr. Anthony De Mello was referring to when he said these words:*

Most people, even though they don't know it, are asleep. They're born asleep, they live asleep, they marry in their sleep, they breed children in their sleep, and they die in their sleep without ever waking up. They never understand the loveliness and the beauty of this thing that we call human existence.

The desire to remain asleep is quite strong; the fact is it's much easier to stay focused on the every day world than it is to pay attention to the whisperings of one's soul. The process of waking up is very unpleasant for most people, because it requires that an individual be willing to seriously question the foundation of his or her entire belief system, including every one of his or her core beliefs about the very nature of existence.

While it may appear easier to just remain asleep, the truth is that avoiding introspection is never beneficial in the long run, for the calling of the soul is very powerful. The more you try to suppress it, the more challenging it becomes to experience true happiness in life. Therefore, the best course of action is to make the effort to wake up, to step outside of your so-called comfort zone, and be willing to explore previously uncharted territory, so that you may ultimately come to an understanding of who you really are. "

Jeff Maziarek (a.k.a. the "Ponder on This" compiler), in "Spirituality Simplified".
www.spiritsimple.com

Relationships: Do you have satisfying relationships with your partner, family, friends, work colleagues, and your community? Do you let them know you appreciate them? Do you terminate relationships that drag you down or damage you? Do you generally enjoy meeting and interacting with other people?

As a species, we're social creatures by nature. Much of the richness in our lives comes from our interactions with other people. Even the shyest among us need some level of engagement with other people.

Home: Do you feel safe, comfortable, and nurtured in your home environment? Do you live in an area that you love? Is your home a peaceful haven, where you're free to be yourself, and able to rest, reflect, and recharge your batteries? Where is 'home' for you?

De-clutter!

We all need a place to which we can retreat after the hustle and bustle of the day. Sometimes it may feel like home is little more than a place to sleep and grab a shower, and the people who you presume are your family or housemates look only vaguely familiar, but your home environment has a significant impact on your overall well-being. There's a big difference between a house and a home.

Work: How satisfied are you at work? Do you love what you do? Do you feel a sense of achievement and contribution? Are you being heard? Do you feel valued? Do you have a role model or a mentor? How much of yourself do you bring to your work?

Most of us spend at least two-thirds of our lives either preparing for work or actually working, and there's no sign that this situation is likely to change anytime soon, indeed it's looking increasingly likely that we will be working even longer hours in the future. It therefore shouldn't come as a total surprise to hear that if we don't feel valued and safe in fully expressing ourselves at work, the quality of our lives is seriously under-mined!

You make your own luck!

Finances: How do you feel about money? Do you lie awake at night worrying about it? Are you aware of your spending habits? Are your finances in order? Do you feel financially secure?

As an intrapreneur, money probably isn't your prime motivator, but as we noted at the outset, it does indeed make the world go round, and can have a significant impact on your quality of life. Taking responsibility for your financial health is one of the best things you can do for yourself.

Mind & body

Relationships

Home

Work

Finances

Meaning & spirituality

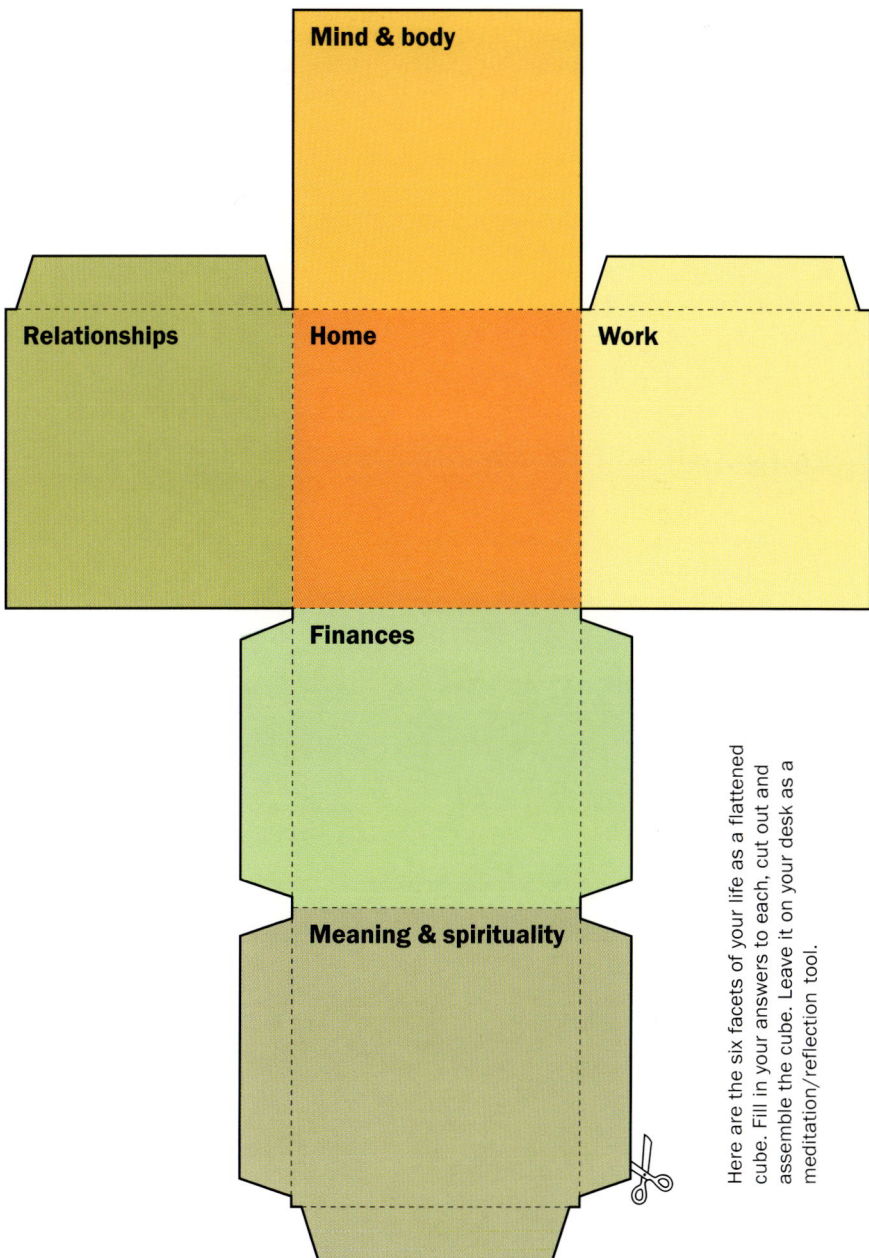

Here are the six facets of your life as a flattened cube. Fill in your answers to each, cut out and assemble the cube. Leave it on your desk as a meditation/reflection tool.

Meaning & spirituality: Is your life meaningful? Do you have a sense of something greater than yourself? Do you have a sense of purpose and direction in your life? What are you grateful for in your life? Do you meditate regularly?

Spirituality gives us a sense of belonging to a world beyond our immediate environment and activities, of being part of a greater force. It's about having faith and hope. Spirituality can provide a peaceful sanctuary, keep us centred, and deliver a sense of calm and stability in times of upheaval and uncertainty.

See the Six Facets of Lisa and Zern on pages 166-167.

Exercise

If you are looking for more meaning and inspiration to wake you up and get the creative juices flowing, why not: paint, sing, draw, dance, write, design, knit, act, build, sculpt, download, photograph, produce, train, nurture, reflect, rejoice, appreciate, cultivate, ponder, muse.

Meet yourself

If you're a naturally introspective and reflective type, meeting yourself should be relatively familiar and easy. If not, you may need to put in some concerted practise.

Here are some tips to help you in the process:

Write separate descriptions of who you are for your partner, your parents, your boss, your kindergarten teacher, your child, and/or your pet. What are the similarities between these descriptions? What are the differences?

Paste your photo here.

Listen to your inner dialogue frequently. What do you say to yourself? Under what circumstances? Can you see a pattern?

What's your perception of yourself as a person? Now talk to people who know you really well, and ask them how they see you. Ask for, and be prepared to receive, honest responses. Do their perceptions align with yours?

What are your boundaries? List all the issues on which you have firm, immoveable beliefs. Is this a long list?

When it comes to generating ideas, are you a black-and-white person, with strict boundaries, or are you a gray person, with lots of flexibility? Creativity requires the latter. You may need to practise being more gray and flexible. It's okay to suspend judgement sometimes, and it's okay to change your mind!

Stay connected with who you are

Spend some time alone every day. Meditate, or just relax and let your thoughts wander.

Think of everything you have for which you're grateful. Each day, make a note of something good that happened. This will help you to maintain a positive frame of mind.

Your future is in your hands.

Continue to learn, grow, and push yourself beyond your comfort zone. Always have an open heart and mind; a desire to achieve your true destiny; persistence; courage to fail and courage to try again; a relentless pursuit of excellence. Be open to opportunities. Remember, they may not even register initially – always be looking to turn challenges into opportunities.

When talking with people, go deeper than simply asking them how they are, or what they do for a living. Share something about your life, and invite them to reciprocate.

Stop being so serious! We're all human, and we all have the same needs.

Every day, take time to scan your body, feelings, thoughts and spirituality. Be guided by your intuition.

Maintain a journal. There are no rules, but if you can write at least four pages at a sitting, you'll get a good insight into your subconscious mind.

Constantly check in with your vision and dreams, and make sure you're on your path towards achieving them. Don't get so caught up in distractions that you wake up in 20 years time and wonder where the hell time has gone and what on earth you're doing!

Reward yourself. Take time out to relax. Pamper yourself. Go on holidays, or do whatever gives you pleasure.

These exercises will help put you in the right frame of mind to maximise your creative potential. Creativity is not something you can turn on and off at will, but by ensuring that you're in good mental and physical shape, you're effectively putting out the welcome mat perchance it should drop by.

Photo: Michelle W

The six facets of Lisa

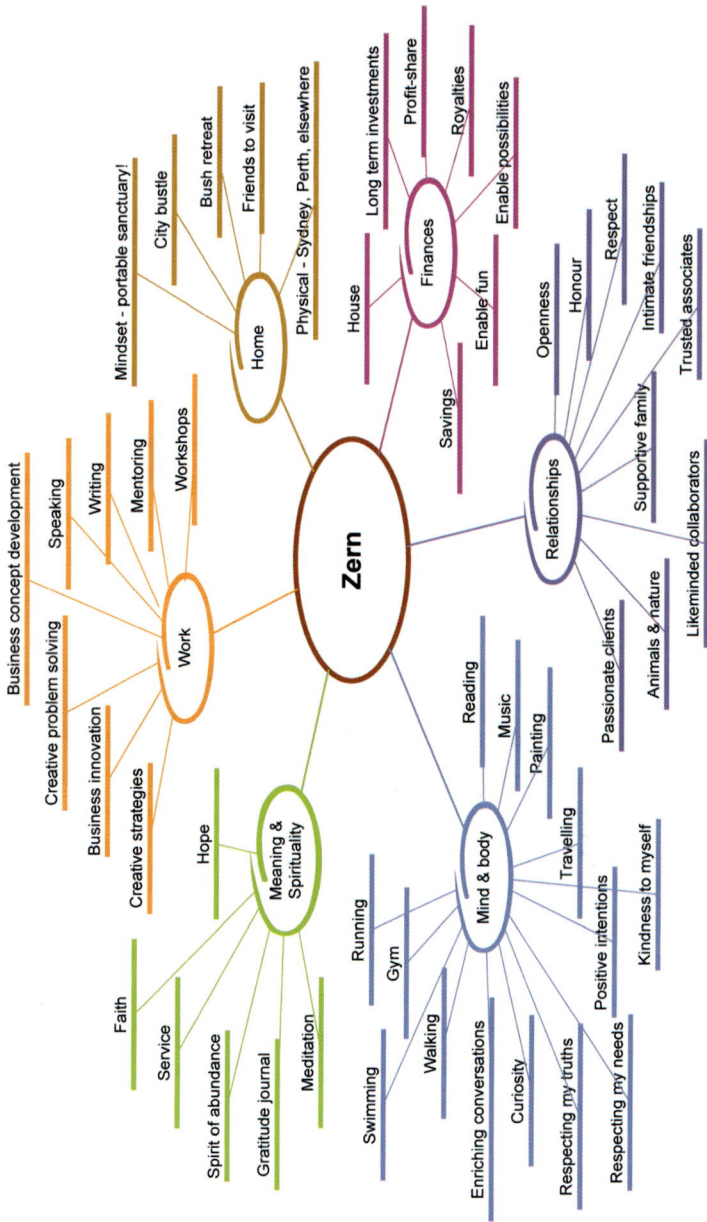

The six facets of Zern

- **Zern**
  - **Home**
    - Mindset - portable sanctuary!
    - City bustle
    - Bush retreat
    - Friends to visit
    - Physical - Sydney, Perth, elsewhere
  - **Finances**
    - Long term investments
    - Profit-share
    - Royalties
    - Enable possibilities
    - Enable fun
    - Savings
    - House
  - **Relationships**
    - Openness
    - Honour
    - Respect
    - Intimate friendships
    - Trusted associates
    - Supportive family
    - Likeminded collaborators
    - Animals & nature
    - Passionate clients
  - **Work**
    - Business concept development
    - Speaking
    - Writing
    - Mentoring
    - Workshops
    - Creative problem solving
    - Business innovation
    - Creative strategies
  - **Meaning & Spirituality**
    - Hope
    - Faith
    - Service
    - Spirit of abundance
    - Gratitude journal
    - Meditation
  - **Mind & body**
    - Reading
    - Music
    - Painting
    - Travelling
    - Kindness to myself
    - Positive intentions
    - Respecting my needs
    - Respecting my truths
    - Curiosity
    - Enriching conversations
    - Walking
    - Swimming
    - Running
    - Gym

How's work?

Let's do an honest assessment of where you are at work:

Are you familiar with the phrase 'work like you don't need the money'? Does that apply to you?

Are you happy with your work, or does it just pay the bills?

Are you content with how you're spending your 40-80 or so hours a week?

Are you resentful?

Do you feel trapped?

Do you feel unimportant?

Is work the enemy? If so, what are you going to do about it?

Is work the most important thing in your life?

Do you value, or devalue, your successes and achievements?

Are you driven by passion, or by duty?

Do you feel challenged and well-rewarded?

Do you feel happy and contented, or sad, depressed, and/or burnt out?

Are you stimulated, and learning new things?

Are you around extraordinary people who appreciate your input, and inspire and excite you with their ideas?

Are you physically fit, or do you eat junk food on the run, sit poorly, and fail to exercise?

Are you creating something useful?

Would you sell it to your grandmother?

Did you choose to be where you are today, or did you fall into it by accident?

Do you now attempt to block out those dreams that have been compromised?

Do you really think this is your lot in life, and it's the best you can do?

A vision for your life

If you want to, you can change the world. But first, you need a compelling vision for your life. You need a reason to get up each morning full of energy and excitement for the challenge ahead. You need a reason for being that inspires people, drawing them closer to you with offers to help out!

Create a vision of how you want your life to be. Remember, this is for your life, not one of your projects! It must include as many aspects of your life as possible. Re-visit the six facets of life section to ensure that you cover all bases.

Think seriously about where you want to be. Lay out the life you desire as a bubble diagram on a sheet of paper. Explore how you feel about what you envision, and invite honest feedback from others.

Focus on your goal with laser precision – you can't get lost on a straight road.

Recognise any negative patterns that are currently controlling your life – over-commitment, jealousy, perfectionism, being a control freak or know-it-all, manipulation, arrogance, fear of success, fear of failure or lack of self-belief.

Think about what you really want in life, and about what you'd like to change.

This should motivate you to move beyond your comfort zone and into a new and exciting place. It's such a simple change, and yet it's amazing how many people are merely living out other peoples dreams and expectations, too caught up in a grinding cycle of 'busyness' to really evaluate who they truly are, and what it is they really want.

Exercise

Manifest what you want. Take a pen and paper and write down your wildest dreams. Imagine not just surviving and doing 'alright', but absolutely living a passionate life that you love.

Remember the child in you – full of fun and spontaneity – does this part of you feel present and acknowledged? How often? Under what situations?

169

What would you do if absolutely anything was possible? So what's stopping you? Remember, it really is – anything is possible! Ask yourself this question: 'What do I want to be remembered for?' What's the one thing that you'd like to be known for? Are you on your way to achieving it right now?

What you need in order to change: (1) Awareness of behavioural patterns, (2) An overwhelming desire to change something in your life, (3) The courage and will to take action.

Fear is an excuse – it's not a reason to give up!

Changing your mind

One of the most valuable lessons you can learn in life is that it's always possible to change your mind! It really is that simple.

So what are your options if you find that the things you believe in are continually being stifled by your organisation? You can try to make changes within the organisation, using all the techniques that have been discussed in this book, or if all else fails, you can simply leave.

Sure, there's usually a price to pay, be it monetary, emotional, or a combination of these. There may be a contract to break, an agreement to renege on, or a friendship to lose. But if your values, your ethics, your satisfaction and your sense of self are being denied, there are obviously significant benefits to be gained as well. If the benefits outweigh the price to be paid, go ahead and change your mind.

There are many paths leading to the same end. You always have a choice. Why not choose to live the life you want?

You always have a choice.

Photo: Luiz Baltar

You are not alone

Remember, you don't have to do this all by yourself. While it's possible for an individual to make a great impact, it's nice to know that there are plenty of great people out there who you can connect with for support and help.

Think about reaching out to innovation consultants and mentors to keep your thinking fresh and your actions on track. Get out there and meet new people. Start participating in discussion forums. Join or start an innovation networking group or attend one of the Cubicle Commando workshops or networking events through www.cubiclecommando.com.au.

You can change the world

Organisations desperately need people like you. Not all of them may know it yet, but their future depends on it. Best to be prepared now!

You can make a huge difference right now simply by deciding to do so – it's in your hands.

It's often said that 'luck' happens when preparation and opportunity collide. With that in mind, we wish you lots of 'luck'.

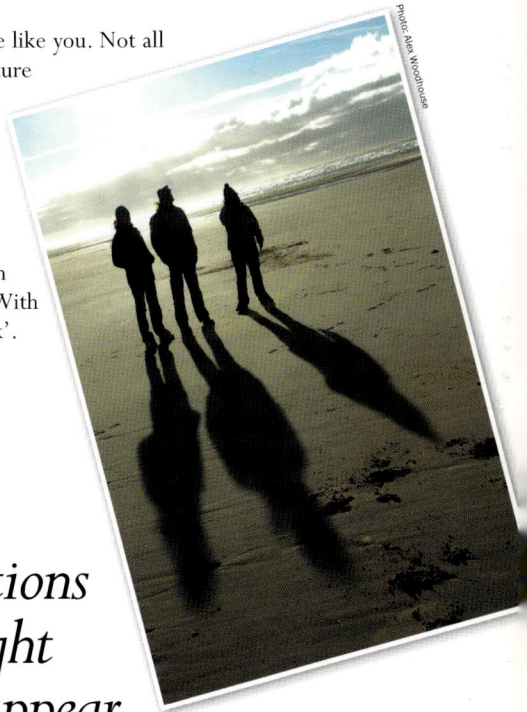

Photo: Alex Woodhouse

If the right questions are asked, the right answers always appear.

Passion

I love the word passion and everything it represents.

Its full of the power to express yourself.

Its about having dreams and chasing them with all your heart.

Its about an indelible inner strength and determination.

People are often fearful of their passions.

They have been programmed into a habitual thinking pattern and as a result live discontented lives.

You can't make positive changes until you realise and own the negative patterns you are perpetuating.

If you don't like what you are doing, change your life and chase your dream now.

What are you waiting for?

Keep striving, never give up, maintain a positive, passionate outlook.

You can take on the world.

Create a new way of living. Change all the rules and you can't go wrong – you will find the strength to do whatever you believe in.

Take risks.

Don't postpone anything for the wrong reasons.

If you believe in it enough you will find a way.

Be tenacious and hold onto your dreams until they become a reality.

Create a vision for yourself. Be in love with life.

Stay true to yourself and your heart.

Use the strength of your passion to become the person you want to be.

Excerpt from *Happiness Is...* by Lisa Messenger

Wellness

is when we have a bounce in our steps,
a feeling of appreciation of life.
It is when we are able to be moved by and are engaged in life...
wellness is when there's lots of laughter around...
and when we feel inspired and have a sense of purpose.
Wellness is also sharing our inspiration with others.
Wellness is being challenged in our work,
but also having an environment in which we can succeed in our challenges.

Things central to wellness are:
balance (work-play, physical/emotional/spiritual wellbeing),
feeling valued and competent,
having opportunities for professional and personal growth
and having the space to celebrate achievements.

Photo: Leah Ciancio

Photo: Lena John

Propelarts exists to propel Youth Arts and Culture in Western Australia. As the peak youth arts body, we offer information, support, audience development, networking, skills development, funding and a collective voice for young creative people and organisations. Wellness is our policy, central to inspiring a vibrant society filled with digital, dance, musical, performance and visual artforms. Propelarts is a mix of no artificial attitudes and plenty of flavour!

www.propelarts.org.au

Other stuff
beyond the back fence

Photo: Zern Liew

RedBalloon

How RedBalloon helps organisations to foster intrapreneurs:

For intrapreneurs, the need for recognition is one of the things that spurs them to continue creating and innovating.

RedBalloon's philosophy is that 'life is the sum of our experiences, not our material goods'. Quite simply, which one are you going to remember the most: the feel of a company pen in your hand, or the feel of the controls of a helicopter as you soar over the city?

It's experiences that form the substance of our lives and are etched forever in our memories. RedBalloon offers vouchers, gift certificates, online programs and group activities to inspire, reward and celebrate successes with your people.

RedBalloon believes that in order to get people thinking creatively, they have to be able to dream. Provide access to those dreams, and you'll unlock the creativity that remains suppressed by the routine nature of corporate life.

www.redballoon.com.au

Here's what people are saying:

Pfizer

"Performance has increased since we began our RedBalloon Days program. We find teams work harder, and they think about their co-workers. You can't put a dollar value on that!"
Kate Hessian

Recoveries Corporation

"The company use RedBalloon Days vouchers to reward truly outstanding achievements by staff. They're still talking today about rewards that individuals took six months ago!"
Sally Thomas

Jet Star

"We implemented the 'Galaxy' program to recognise our star performers, whereby team mates and managers nominate one another for a RedBalloon Days voucher. The enthusiasm and encouragement throughout the team is evident." Rohan Garnett

Always carry this book with you. Stay true to yourself. Leverage the power of business for good. Remember the "power of AND". Subversion is important. Fight mediocrity. Ideas and concepts rule. Tap into your feminine side. Unleash your passions. Be a part of the revolution. Adopt a new mindset. Have passion, creativity and the desire to make a difference. Make meaning from your work. Be yourself. Be extraordinary. Act with integrity. Live your personal brand. Be curious – about everything. Find and get behind your cause. Stand up for yourself. Get into the action. Be optimistic. Engage with like-minded people. Be a mover and shaker. Ask why. Think as big as you can and go for it. Know what fear smells like, take a deep breath and do it anyway. Be a dreamer, thinker, doer in one. Be kind to yourself. You always have a choice.

Recognise the power of working with others. Live through your heart and soul. Create buy-in with involvement. Convert enemies to allies. Engage through vision. Create your intraprise. Live your dream. Have big, hairy, audacious goals. Be open and accepting. Create suspense and mystery. Reward yourself and your team. Be open to all possibilities. Listen to your intuition. Don't follow fashion. Be agile and adaptable. Create an 'anti-process' process. Embrace constraints. Leverage systems. Pick your battles. Accept the things you cannot change. Value and acknowledge yourself. Know what you want. Ask for what you want. Know what success means to you. Make your own luck. Stay true to who you are. Create a vision for your life. You are an intrapreneur. You can change the world. You are not alone.

"Now get out there and create, innovate and live the life you are meant to!"

Lisa & Zern

"*There is always more than one way to do anything!*"

About Lisa Messenger

Lisa has worked globally in conference and event management, PR, sponsorship, marketing and publishing. She is the Managing Director of Messenger Marketing and Messenger Publishing and Co-Director of Anchovy Publishing.

She has also authored and published *Happiness Is...* and is currently working on several other titles including a novel; a cookbook for Peppers Hotels and a book, CD and DVD set on self publishing titled *Maverick Publishing* – a phrase she has recently coined.

She is also featured in books by Robyn Henderson, The NSW Department of Primary Industries and the Department for Women.

Lisa writes extensively for a number of magazines, and has had regular stints on radio and the occasional TV appearance. She is a judge for the Australian Business and Specialist Publishers' national Bell Awards, sits on the board of the Australian Businesswomen's Network and chaired the 2006 International Women's Day for them in Australia. She also sits on the Tomorrows Youth Board and the Theatrelab Board.

She is also an active supporter of charities Kids Help Line and Opportunity International.

Never one to be constrained by traditions and conventions, her passion, imagination, creativity, energy and business flair have led her on many fun and outrageous adventures. Thriving on challenges, smashing barriers and taking people beyond their comfort zone is what drives Lisa's "nothing's impossible" approach.

She is now using her unique marketing talents and innovative approach with entrepreneurs, intrapreneurs and people all over the globe.

Her passion is to challenge individuals and corporations to change the way they think, take them out of their comfort zone and prove that there is more than one way to do anything.

lisa@messengermarketing.com.au

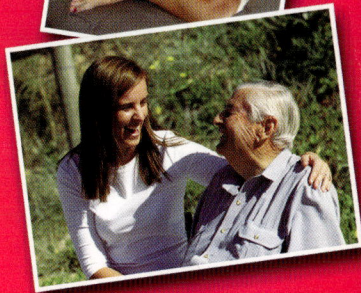

About Zern Liew

Zern is a creative strategist and innovation facilitator.

He uses his diverse skills to enable entrepreneurs and businesses to grow towards their full potential and meet business challenges effectively and creatively. He is passionate about bringing humanity, community and authenticity to the practice of business.

He has over ten years experience as a multidisciplinary designer, information architect, business concept innovator, business process architect, lateral problem-solver, e-media producer and software developer.

He works with passionate individuals to draw out the answers within them; to illuminate the possibilities in each challenge; to see clear paths forward amidst distractions; and develop innovative and appropriate outcomes to meet every challenge.

He has worked on projects with a wide range of clients including: AMP, Australian Chamber Orchestra, Australian Major Performing Arts Group, Citibank Seoul, Commonwealth Department of Finance and Administration, Fender Australia, IBM Australia, Institute of Chartered Accountants in Australia, Liverpool City Council, Merck Sharpe & Dohme, MLC, National Gallery of Australia, News Limited, Opera Australia, and the Sydney 2000 Olympic Games.

In addition to consulting and design work, Zern also volunteers his professional services to charities, speaks to high school students, mentors entrepreneurs, and writes articles on business practice on FlyingSolo.com.au. He has been written about in the Sydney Morning Herald, GoodCompany and MyBusiness magazine.

zern@eicolab.com

Innovation = playful creativity + business realities

Business is the most powerful world-shaping force today; changing the world means changing business practice. Business is about people; changing business practice starts with you and me!

Ideas, vision, courage, truth, and integrity matters more than ever before in business.
I am doing my bit to help
businesses get there.

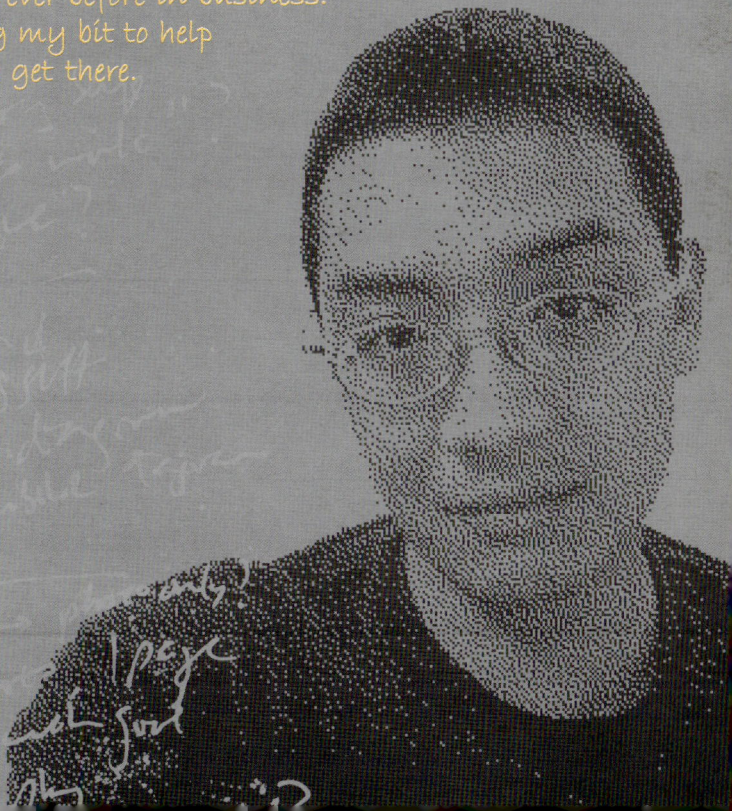

Thank

Lisa

In 2003 I did The Hoffman Process - a profound eight-day roller coaster ride a la Freud meets Walt Disney. It was a wake up call and the beginning of a new world and a new life for me. Since then, incredible, amazing and awe-inspiring things have happened in my life and I am extraordinarily thankful to have been surrounded by inspirational, optimistic, creative and passionate people who have mentored and guided me in so many ways – many of whom make appearances in their own special way in, and others who have been supportive of, this book.

So, for just being, I would like to thank:

Sally Muller – a truly beautiful soul and someone I am proud to have as a best friend.

Kate Messenger – a constant bundle of joy and inspiration – my sister soul mate.

John Messenger – for being brave enough to change course later in life.

Sir John Fuller – for his constant belief in my crazy ideals which are often diametrically opposed to his due to generational gaps, but somehow we both managed and are managing to innovate for our time, and therefore have a common interest in making a difference and debating the tides of change.

Lady Fuller – for your dignity, humour, cheekiness and un-wavering strength.

Bryan, **Margot**, **Rachel** and **Claire Fuller** for being the superstar cheerleaders.

Paul Morris for the invaluable discussions and brainstorming sessions. You are a true entrepreneur, visionary, and extraordinary friend.

The best friends anyone could wish for – **Kate Bezar**, **Kris McIntyre**, **Trish Harding**, **Hayley Crossing**, **Steph Ridgeway**, **Meegan Cornforth**, **Gina Chapman**, **Simone Cobb**, **Donna Aboody**, **Scotty Grimster**, **Erin Campbell**, **Bella Finlayson**, **Andrew Hose**, **Simone Cobb** and **Dunc Steele Park**.

My post Pinquers – **Darain Faraz**, **Sonya Georges**, **Mandy Higgins**.

My wonderful clients and colleagues from whom I gain so much inspiration and learn so much – Steve Fenton, Paul Gordon, Suzi Dafnis, Amy Lyden, Belinda Yabsley, Suzy Yates, Volker Khron, Matt Church, Chris Gray, Nils Vesk, Brooke Alexander, Oksana Koriakova, Simone Tregeagle, Russell Jeffery, Kathy Williams, Ingrid Mogenson, Craig Rispin, Ross Cameron, Phil Black, Marcus and Mel West, Julie Winterbottom, Dr Tim Sharp, Maurice Goldberg and Hailey Cavill.

you

Together, we would like to thank these people who have supported our journey with Cubicle Commando:

Geoff Whyte – a true partnership with an editor extraordinaire. One of the funniest and most talented people we could have possibly wished for on the team.

Adam Crouch, Ed Peterie and **Kristy Allen, Peter Murray.**

Bryan Fuller and **Trish Harding** – for modelling Gary and Trinity.

Rachel Fuller – photography of Trinity, Gary and the authors. And all the other photographers who have generously shared their wonderful images with us.

Our contributors who so generously shared their stories of inspiration and innovation: Chip Conley - Joie de Vivre Hospitality, **Siimon Reynolds** – Love, **Paul Gordon** – ipac, **Chris Warrell** – Australand, **Andrew McEvoy** – Tourism Australia, **Kate Bezar** – Dumbo feather, **Matt Church** – Thought Leaders, **Glenn Capelli** – True Learning Centre, **Robert Gerrish** – Flying Solo, **Toby Marshall** – Abacus, **Andrew Ward** – 3 Minute Angels, **Lena John** – Propelarts, and **David Egan.**

And all those who are a constant source of inspiration to us: Tom Peters, Richard Branson, Anita Roddick, Steve Jobs, Chip Conley, Jonas Ridderstrale, Kjell Nordström, Bono, Oprah Winfrey, and **Guy Kawasaki.**

Zern

My mum and dad **Ngok Yin** and **Fui En** for giving me all the opportunities, for having faith in me to seek out and live the life I need to live, and for introducing me to books.

Helen Richards for being the best friend and muse anyone could ask for. I would not be the person I am without your insights, generosity, and kindness.

Jeff Cahill for teaching me how to be real; to honour the unfettered big dreams while at the same time embracing the pragmatic possibilities in reality.

Martin Apte for being the most inspiring intrapreneur I have ever met; for showing me it is possible to do the right thing, be real, AND be successful.

Bettina Cutler for your big vote of confidence back in '98 that propelled me to strike out on my own, and for your ongoing belief in me, and for all your support.

Bede Tannock and **Sandra Di Bartolomeo** for your friendship and belief in me; and for the bad horrors, good wine and long lazy Perth days.

Stilgherrian for being one of the most perceptive and honourable people I have had the opportunity to learn from.

Bruce Thompson for making me laugh when the going got tough, and the wheels threaten to fall off my yum cha trolley.

Christina Jayne Duncan for helping me find and stay true to my truths. And for your music.

Greg Ralph, Natalie Shell, Michael Chang, Lynette Dean and **Mark Montanet** for your kind thoughts throughout this process.

Will Fraser, Amanda Smith, Noel Lenehan, Craig Garratt, Lars Rasmussen, Dic Liew and **Paul Cutler** for so patiently and generously putting up with my many questions.

Biographies

Beatty, Jack. *The World According to Peter Drucker*. New York, Free Press, 1998.

Branson, Richard. *Losing My Virginity. How I've Survived, Had Fun and Made a Fortune Doing Business My Way.* New York, Random House, 1998.

Dearlove, Des and Stuart Crainer. *Business the Richard Branson Way: 10 Secrets of the World's Greatest Brand-Builder.* New York: AMACOM, 1999.

Drucker, Peter Ferdinand. *The Effective Executive.* New York: Harper Business, 1993.

Freiberg, Kevin and Jackie Freiberg. *Nuts! Southwest Airlines' Crazy Recipe for Business and Personal Success.* Austin, Tex: Bard Press, 1996.

Iverson, Ken. *Plain Talk: Lessons from a Business Maverick.* New York: Wiley, 1998.

Jackson, Tim. *Richard Branson: Virgin King.* Rocklin, Calif: Prima Publishing, 1996.

Mandela, Nelson. *Long Walk to Freedom*, Abacus 2004.

Roddick, Anita. *Body and Soul.* Ebury Press, 1991.

Schulz, Howard. *Pour Your Heart into It: How Starbucks Build a Company One Cup at a Time.* New York: Hyperion, 1997.

Self Empowerment and Personal Growth

Bolles, Richard Nelson. *What Colour is Your Parachute?* New York: Ten Speed Press, 1991.

Kotter, P. John. *The New Rules: Eight Business Breakthroughs to Career Success in the 21st Century.* New York: Free Press Paperbacks, 1995.

McGrath, John. *You inc. : how to attract amazing success into your life and business.* HarperCollins, 2003.

Messenger, Lisa. *Happiness Is….* Sydney. Messenger Publishing. 2004.

Miller, Alice. *The Drama of the Gifted Child: The Search for the True Self.* New York: Harper Perennial, 1997

Ziegler, Mel; Will Rosenzweig; and Patricia Ziegler. *The Republic of Tea: Letters to a Young Zentrepeneur.* New York: Currency / Doubleday, 1992.

Inspirational, Creativity and Empowerment

Barrett, Richard. *Liberating the Corporate Soul: Building a Visionary Organisation.* New York: Butterworth-Heinemann, 1998.

Barez-Brown, Chris. *How to Have Kick-Ass Ideas: Get Curious, Get Adventurous, Get Creative.* Harper Element, 2006.

Bono; *Bono on Bono – Conversations with Michka Assayas*, Hodder, 2005.

Bradford, David and Allan R Cohen. *Power Up, Transforming Organisations Through Shared Leadership.* New York: Wiley, 1998.

Cameron, Julia. *The Artists Way: A Spiritual Path to Higher Creativity.* New York: Putnam, 1992.

Church, Matt. *High Life 24/7*. ABC Books, 2004.

Gray, Chris. *Go For Your Life*. Pennon 2005.

Heskett, James L; Earl W Sasser and Leonard A Schlesinger. *The Service Profit Chain: How Leading Companies Link Profit and Growth to Loyalty, Satisfaction and Value*. New York: Free Press, 1997.

James, Geoffrey. *Success Secrets from Silicon Valley: How to Make Your Teams More Effective (No Matter What Business You're In)*: New York, Times Business, 1998.

Laurence, Tim. *You Can Change Your Life: A Future Different from Your Past with The Hoffman Process,* Great Britain: Hodder Headline, 2003.

Nelson, Bob. *1001 Ways to Reward Your Employees*. New York: Workman Publishing Co, 1994

Sharp, Dr Timothy. *The Happiness Handbook – Strategies for a Happy Life*. Finch Publishing, 2005.

Sinetar, Marsha. *Do What you Love, the Money Will Follow*. New York: Paulist Press, 1987.

Small Business

Gerber, Michael. *The E Myth Revisited: Why Most Small Businesses Don't Work and What to Do About It*. New York: Harper Collins, 1995.

Gerrish, Robert and Sam Leader. *Flying Solo - How to go it alone in business*. Allen & Unwin, 2005.

Godin, Seth. *The Bootstrapper's Bible. How to Start and Build a Business with a Great Idea and (Almost) No Money*. Chicago: Dearborn Financial Publishing, 1998.

Management

Ridderstrale, Jonas and Kjelle Nordstrom. *Funky Business: Talent Makes Capital Dance*. Prentice Hall, 2002.

Marketing

Godin, Seth. *Permission Marketing*. New York: Simon & Schuster, 1999.

Chaston, Ian. *Entrepreneurial Marketing: Competing by Challenging Convention*. MacMillan Business, 2000.

Rebels in Corporations

Conley, Chip. *The Rebel Rules: Daring to Be Yourself in Business*. Simon & Schuster, 2001.

Kleiner, Art. *The Age of Heretics: Heroes, Outlaws, and the Forerunners of Corporate Change*. New York: Currency / Doubleday, 1996.

Lee, William. *Mavericks in the Workplace*. New York: Oxford University Press, 1998.

Southon, Mike and Chris West. *The Boardroom Entrepreneur*. Random House, 2005.

What If! *Sticky Wisdom: How to Start a Creative Revolution at Work*. Capstone, 2002.

RedBalloon DAYS
Amazing Gifts for Amazing People

Shake up your intrapreneurship!

Lisa Messenger and Zern Liew are available to assist corporates and individuals foster intrapreneurship and innovation.

We work with you on a one-on-one consultancy basis to develop your ability to innovate at work or to solve specific problems creatively.

We can also be engaged to run internal half and full-day innovation and creativity workshops.

We also take on a select few people as private mentoring clients, assisting them to reach their full potential as dynamic intrapreneurs.

Find out more about Cubicle Commando-related products, services and material at www.cubiclecommando.com.au

If you know someone who is an extraordinary intrapreneur or entrepreneur with a story worth telling, we would love to hear from you or them for possible inclusion in upcoming books.

Lisa Messenger – lisa@messengermarketing.com.au

Zern Liew – zern@eicolab.com

Messenger
Publishing

About The Messenger Group: Messenger Marketing & Messenger Publishing

The Messenger Group encompasses a creative and innovative publishing and marketing consultancy that thrives on lateral thinking to create out of the box solutions for our clients. We are **never** limited by conventions and traditional approaches and love to invoke attitudinal shift to make extraordinary things happen.

Our mission is to make the dreams and goals of our clients come alive. We are passionate about having fun and let our imaginations soar beyond predictable solutions, demonstrating that there is always more than one way to do anything. We love helping people to make a difference, leverage their ability and stand up for what they believe in.

We are experts in innovation across a number of industries – with publishing being one that we've recently shaken up in a big way. We have developed a model that enables corporates and individuals to produce custom books that can become a credible, lasting extension of your brand; an integral part of your existing marketing mix and an additional source of revenue.

www.messengermarketing.com.au

"I love Lisa's ability to think creatively. She holds the rare ability to do this at the Strategic level. I think she is a dynamo, and would say that if you need thorough, well considered marketing and publishing strategies, she is the one. Her next big thing will certainly be in shaking up the 'establishment' industries. A real cattle prod!"
– Matt Church, Owner, Thought Leaders and leading expert of personal leadership

"Lisa's publishing and marketing genius has completely changed my thinking on book publishing. As a successful international author, I thought I knew the best way to publish, but since working with Lisa I have realised that there are a lot better ways to publish and market books without having to rely on the publishing giants. Thanks Lisa."
– Nils Vesk , Director, Life's Little Tool Box

"Lisa is a business woman with abundant energy and potential. She is not afraid to take risks and try new strategies and has an amazing way of coming up with ideas that are completely unique. Lisa gives freely of her time to speak to our small business students on a regular basis and sits on our panel for the New Enterprise Incentive Scheme"
– David Baumgarten, CEO, Eastern Suburbs Business Enterprise Centre

"It is rare to find someone courageous enough to challenge old ways of thinking and doing – especially in a major industry such as publishing. Even rarer to find someone who then shares their learning's with other people – with honesty and modesty. Lisa Messenger is that rare person. She has found a better way to get important messages into the marketplace through books in all their glorious & unique forms, and she is imparting that knowledge to aspiring authors such as myself via her fantastic one-day workshops. I came away not only knowing that I will do it, but how to do it, as well as knowing that there is an expert only a phone call away. Lisa you are an inspiration!"
– Hailey Cavill, Director, Cavill and Co